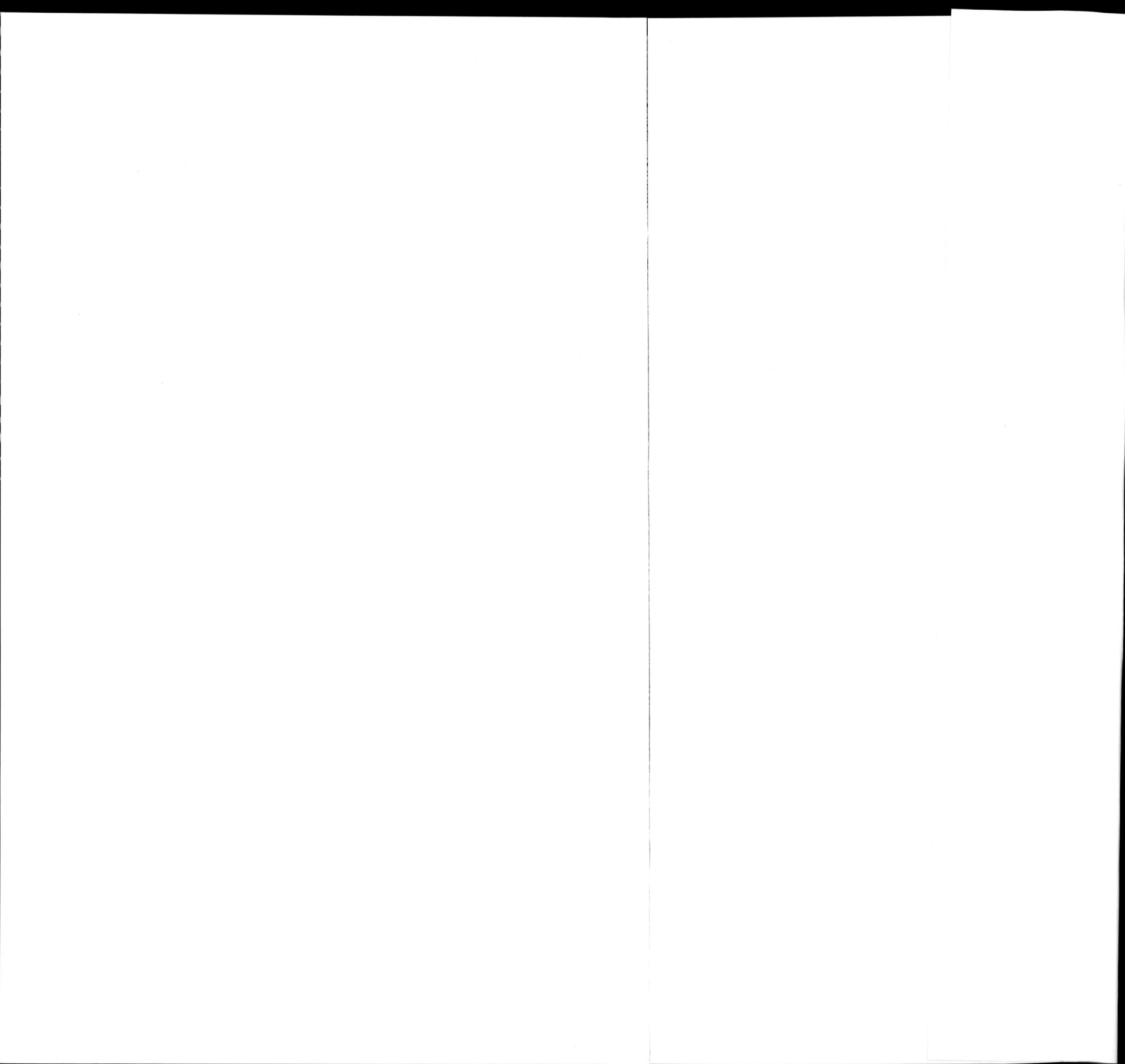

MOONSHINE DAYS

The Century Old Story of
Robert Lee Swindell

By Susan D. Brandenburg

Copyright on all of the work is held by Carlton H.
Spence; nevertheless, grateful acknowledgement is
made to Author Susan D. Brandenburg, to Robert Lee
Swindell for graciously sharing his remarkable life,
and to all those who contributed their thoughts and
memories to this book.

ISBN: 978-0-9973135-5-0

Layout and Design by
Philip Barnes
Riverducks Design
riverducksdesign@gmail.com

TABLE OF CONTENTS

PREFACE

He was thin, wiry, and strong. At age 11, Robert's angular face had a stone-hard solemn look of determination about it. His dark piercing eyes discouraged casual conversation. Robert Swindell was not afraid of anything ... anything except that old, one-eyed black man waiting for him deep in the woods.

Robert's breath caught in his throat. He could hear that old man talking to himself ... grumbling in a low, mean growl. "Where the hell is that no-good white boy? I need my firewood .... I need it now!"

Holding tight to the bunch of dry limbs he'd been dragging through the woods, Robert began running toward the gruff voice as fast as he could. When he finally appeared in the clearing, old one-eye just glared at him and motioned toward the fire-pit. "Well, don't just stand there, boy. Put the wood down and get me some more!"

Robert didn't know which was worse ... prowling around in the woods searching for firewood or sitting on a log in the shadows watching the old man make moonshine. Fingering the shiny 50 cent piece in his pocket, he backed into the eerie darkness. The deal was that he wouldn't get picked up until sunrise.

"Ah hell," he thought, cautiously reaching into the brush for what he hoped was a dry limb instead of a black snake. "I'd sooner get bit by a snake than go back empty-handed and have old one-eye put some kind of voodoo spell on me."

This was one of many nights Robert would spend searching the forest for firewood to keep the moonshine operation going. He soon learned how to make the shine himself, and he learned never to turn his back on that mean old one-eyed black man.

INTRODUCTION

I met Robert Swindell shortly after the marriage of his daughter, Darlene, to my son, Jeff. Throughout the years and even up until now I have enjoyed the many stories of his life. His eyes always seem to particularly light up when he tells tales about his moonshining days. He talks of the danger of being deep in the dark woods and gathering dry limbs all night long for the mean old one-eyed black man who tended the firebox for the Still. He recalls the excitement of running from revenuers – both on foot and in fast cars. It is apparent that he was a boy with avid curiosity and ambition who loved the jingle of moonshine money in his pockets but was always on the lookout for ways to make an honest dollar. Robert is a man with a past worth remembering. As the days and weeks go by there are fewer men and women left who can convey the interesting facts of this bygone era. I hope Robert has many more years to generate new inspiring happenings, however, the time is now to record and celebrate his 101st birthday.

Carlton H. Spence
May 2017

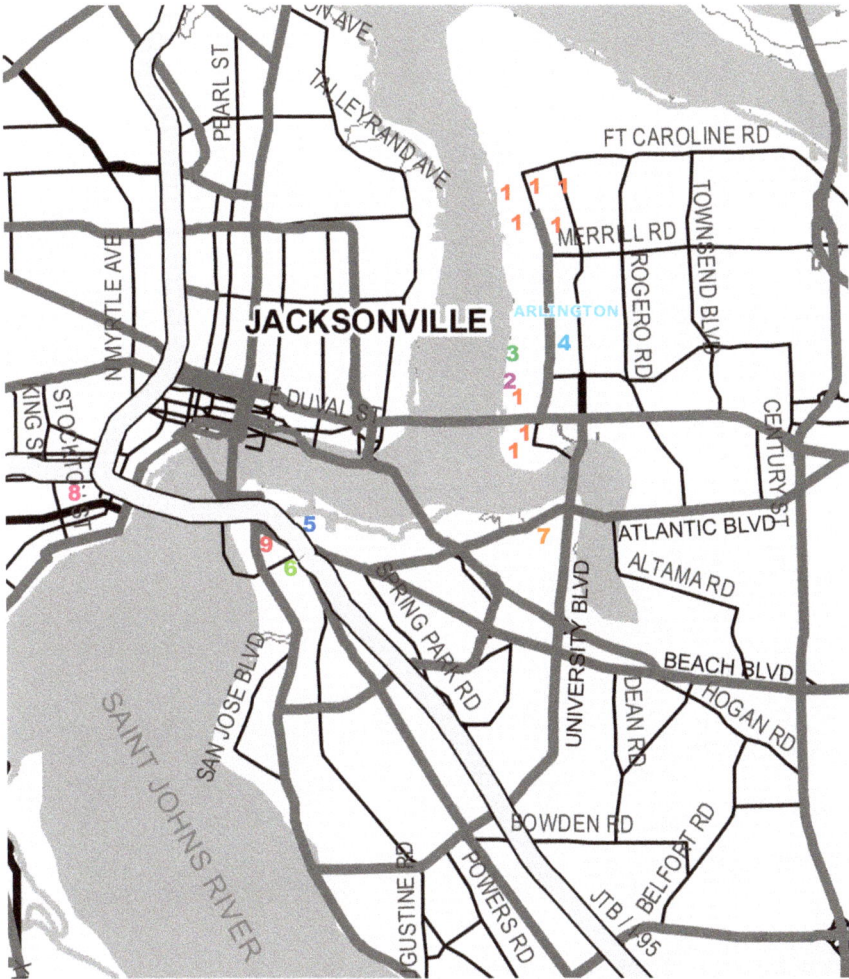

1 Approx. locations of stills in the 1920s/1930s (there were others)

2 J. Olson Marine Corp. (home of Julius & Emma) from 1900s to 1970s

3 Robert and Gladys's first house (1938)

4 Robert and Gladys's second house (late 1945)

5 1106 Bee Street (Home) $4500 in late 1945

6 Eva's (Robert's mother) store on Kings Ave. (now US1) late 20s/early 30s

7 Atlantic Drive-In

8 Deliveries of moonshine to Riverside/Avondale

9 Landon High School (site of Up & Up Club) 8th and 9th grades

CHAPTER 1
BOYHOOD

When 100-year-old Robert Lee Swindell looks back on his long, eventful life, some days remain vivid in his memory. Tales of his dangerous, exciting "Moonshine Days" as a youth in Jacksonville, Florida have been told and retold over the years and now those fascinating stories belong to you, the reader of this book.

But before we head for the still in the woods where the old one-eyed black man lurks, and begin to savor the taste of that wild white lightning, let's go back to the beginning and tell you about the boy who inspired this book.

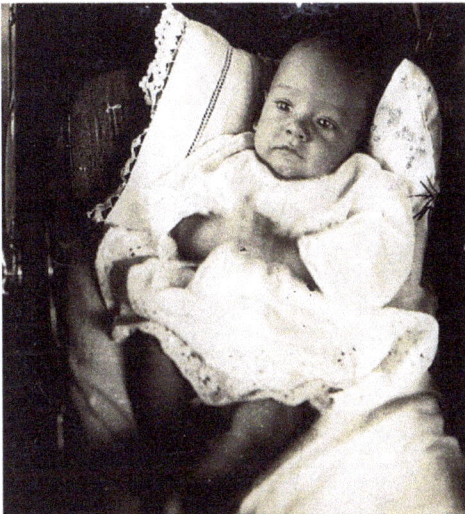

Robert Lee Swindell

He was born to Robert David and Eva Annise Swindell on May 15, 1916 in Watertown, just south of Lake City, Florida.

**Robert with his parents,
Eva and Robert David Swindell**

Until 1859, Lake City had been the site of a former Seminole Indian village named Alpata Telophka, meaning "Alligator Village." When the city was incorporated in 1859, it is said the mayor's wife refused to hang her lace curtains in a town named Alligator, so it was renamed Lake City because of the local bodies of water in its vicinity. These include Lake DeSoto, Lake Isabella, Alligator Lake, Lake Hamburg, Gwen Lake, Lake Harper and Watertown Lake.

The Civil War Battle of Olustee took place just east of Lake City in February 1864, the only major battle fought in Florida during the war, and Lake City's centennial was celebrated in 1959 with parades and fireworks and a book titled

Robert David & Robert Lee Swindell

"A Century in the Sun," but for our purposes, the most interesting item of Lake City history is all about the "Moon … shine."

Robert's grandparents, both maternal and paternal, were from the Lake City area and, like their descendant, lived long and colorful lives.

Robert's paternal grandmother, Janie (Yarbrough) Swindell, carried in her pocket a small handle 32 Smith & Wesson Pistol. She said it was to kill "critters" (never designating whether they were of the four-legged or two-legged variety). That gun (probably about

Robert David Swindell, Railroad Foreman

150 years old now) has been handed down to Zach Swindell, Robert's great-grandson. Sadly, Janie lost her son, Robert David Swindell, in 1924, at Lacoochee, Florida. Robert David, only 35 at the time of his death, was a railroad foreman like his father, Doc. It is ironic, indeed, considering the name and subject of this book

and the memories created by Robert Lee Swindell's connection to moonshine, that his father died of lead poisoning directly related to drinking a bad batch of moonshine.

Young Robert Lee was just seven years old and his sister, Mildred, five, when their Dad died, and their Mother, Eva, had to go to work to support her young family.

Mildred and Robert

Grandmother Janie, who lived near Lake City in Anthony, Florida often took care of Robert and Mildred when Eva was working in Palatka or Tampa, or as far away as New Jersey. Robert remembers helping his grandmother do laundry on Mondays and learning from her how to cook beans. "She always had a pot of beans on the fire," he recalls, adding, "I have cooked a lot of beans in my life!"

As to his maternal grandparents, Mathew and Lily Howard lived in Lake City and also occasionally took care of their grandkids, Robert and Mildred, while Eva worked long hours, long miles away, at one time moving to New Jersey to work for a doctor. She made good money and sent it home to care for the children, but had little time to spend with them personally. Robert would later state that he basically raised himself and would not let that happen to his children. He did, however, enjoy those days with the Howards … days often spent listening to the exciting tales of his great-granddad, old Floyd Thornton Harper, who could recall Civil War battles and years gone by when Lake City was once known as Alligator Village.

At ages 7 and 8, Robert was already developing a love for the written word and, encouraged by his grandparents, he would find a quiet spot and read any book he could get his hands on. Adventure stories were his favorites. Robinson Crusoe, by Daniel Defoe, The Three Musketeers, by Alexandre Dumas, and Treasure Island, by Robert Louis Stevenson were some of the books he loved. He also read books about cowboys and the old West. Robert dreamed of traveling to faraway places that he read about in books.

"Mama was always working when I was a boy," Robert says, "and I don't remember Dad, except one time I seem to remember him bringing me a baseball bat to take to the playground." He got most of his elementary schooling in Tampa, where they lived right across the street from the school. His mother worked for a while at the restaurant next door and that was where they ate their meals, too. When he came home from school, Robert would sit on the front porch and read and watch what was happening in the neighborhood. He's always been an avid observer of people and nature.

Sometimes he and friends would sit on the porch and try to catch birds. They'd throw out corn and the birds would flock to get it and then they would reach down and grab a bird. "Them damn birds. I caught a big old Blue Jay! Had hold of him and got my hands under his wings and let his wings out. I was looking at this bird and then I turned him so he was looking at me. I could see fire in his eyes. I messed with him a while longer and let him go." Robert understood the fire in the bird's eyes ... he didn't like being confined in a small space either.

Another day, he was sitting on the front porch alone when he saw the school bully come out on the sidewalk and grab the doctor's son. "He grabbed him and they fell down. I got off the porch and went down and got into it," he recalls. "I pulled the bully off, pushed him hard, and helped him get across the street. He hauled ass, shaking his fist at me and yelling, 'I'll get you!' but he never came across the street again."

Independent and self-taught, even as a young boy Robert had keen powers of observation and could usually grasp a situation and handle it. Looking back, it is obvious that he ached for affection from his busy, distracted mother, but her lack of guidance and concern was probably one of the reasons that Robert became determined early on to learn all he could and fend for himself.

For instance, when they moved to Jacksonville, Florida, and an elderly man took him out fishing for the first time, he learned quickly. "One of the fellows we were with got sick and we had to take him in," Robert remembers. "After that, I didn't need him or anybody else to go fishing. I knew how to do it. I had a cane pole and worms and I bought hooks. I watched other fishermen – saw what they were doing and did it myself. How they rigged their poles and rods and reels … you see what they're doing and then do what they're doing … that's the way life works." He taught his children to fish the same way.

From about the time he was 11 years old, Robert was an avid fisherman who considered fishing serious business rather than sport. "Whether or not you're a good fisherman depends on the fish," he says. "I've fished enough to consider myself a fisherman, but if the fish don't bite, you aren't going to catch them!"

Although she doesn't know the basis for this legend, Darlene remembers her dad always saying, "If cows are lying down in the pasture, there's no need to even go out. The fish aren't biting."

Their move to Jacksonville was precipitated by Robert's mother, Eva, finding a job at Western Union and eventually buying a little store on Kings Avenue. There is very little written about Robert's sister, Mildred, whom he loved and respected. She was a beautiful girl and Robert remembers being quite protective of his baby sister. "The boys knew not to mess with her because they knew about me!" he says, shaking his clenched fist.

Another reason for Eva moving her family to Jacksonville after her husband died was that she was dating a man named Rutland "Rut" Aderhold. "Mama knew he was a 'Shiner,'" Robert recalls. "I guess they made good money. I got along with him alright. I knew what they were doing was illegal, but Mama wasn't around and they offered us boys 50 cents apiece for helping them."

Robert came home from school one day, did his chores and homework and then Rut dropped him off by the woods to gather firewood for the old black man who ran the still. "I started when somebody else didn't show up," Robert says. "I took his place and I did a fairly good job of it so after that I had the job." Doing a "fairly good job" of dragging dead limbs through the woods to that scary old one-eyed black man took a lot of nerve for the little 11-year-old, but Robert was tough and resilient. He'd drag the branches until his arms were aching and no matter how quick he was, the old man would yell at him to go back and get more for the firebox ... Fast, boy, Fast!" Robert could tell when he was mad – he stayed mad. Scattering frantically through the woods, as dusk turned to dark, the boy searched for dry limbs first with his feet and then with his hands, hoping against hope that he wouldn't pick up a snake instead of a stick. As the night dragged on, he realized that he had been there for hours and he was hungry and cold and tired. He smelled some kind of meat cooking at the old man's campfire … he finally snuck back to the edge of the clearing and sat on a log, watching and waiting. He knew better than to ask for a taste of whatever the old man was cooking. His stomach growled, and he hugged his knees, shivering. When would Rut come to pick him up? Did he forget about him? His eyes began to feel heavy and he drifted off to an uneasy sleep, crouching there on that log in the woods. When he awoke, early morning sunlight was shooting through the tree branches above his head and Rut was shaking his shoulder. "C'mon boy, wake up. It's time to get ready for school."

Yes, doing a "fairly good job" that first night of his moonshine days marked a turning point in his life. Although he knew what he was doing was illegal, Robert found that the excitement and danger of it was intoxicating. That was the night that Robert Lee Swindell's boyhood came to an end … he had turned a corner and embarked on a new, unfamiliar path. Where it would take him, he did not know.

CHAPTER 2
SCHOOL AND SHINE

After his early initiation into the Moonshine business, Robert did his best to maintain some semblance of boyhood while enjoying the jingle of 50 cent pieces in his pockets from frequent forays into the woods of Jacksonville's Arlington and Southside areas. Those were the days of the Great Depression (early 1930's) and it sure did feel good to have some actual money that he could spend as he chose.

His mother, Eva, had married Rut Aderhold. Rut ran moonshine and Eva ran her little grocery and mercantile store on Kings Avenue. Robert and his buddies would meet after school at the store and skate up Kings Avenue to Times Square (where U.S. 1 and Atlantic Blvd. met). Sometimes they'd skate up Atlantic Blvd. to the fountain in San Marco and then back to the store on Kings Avenue, right in the middle of the street. There were trolley cars that ran up and down Atlantic Boulevard, making the turn at the circle in San Marco. When the trolley stopped, the boys sometimes would sneak up and put a penny on the rail and grease the rails so the wheels of the trolley just spun and there was no traction. The conductor would come out and cuss at the boys for what they'd done. The boys, laughing as hard as they could laugh, ended up with a flattened penny and an angry conductor.

Rarely would they encounter a car as they skated those roads that are now so heavily trafficked and interspersed with stop signs and stoplights. Skating as fast as they could go, laughing and yelling back and forth, daring one another to skate on one foot or take a long leap over a curb, the boys were the picture of carefree youth ... but a dark cloud hovered over one of them and that cloud was the secret he kept to himself ... Robert Swindell was a bootlegger ... a moonshiner ... a criminal ... and he knew it.

The term "bootlegger" came from colonial times when smugglers rode on horseback with liquor concealed in their high riding boots, but in the 1920's and 30's, bootleggers transported illegal alcohol brewed by moonshiners in home-made distilleries (stills) hidden deep in wooded areas. The manufacturing and distributing of "beer, wine, or other intoxicating malt or vinous liquors" had been made illegal in the United States by passage of the 18th Amendment, known as the National Prohibition Act of 1919. The 18th Amendment gave power to the Commissioner of Internal Revenue, his assistants, agents and inspectors, to enforce the illegality of moonshining (so-called because the liquor was made late at night by the light of the moon). Moonshiners didn't pay taxes on the liquor they produced and sold. That was another issue that made it illegal and a matter for the Commissioner of the Internal Revenue.

During those prohibition years (1919 to 1933) and beyond, a fierce battle was waged by the "Revenuers" against the Moonshiners and Bootleggers, making the brewing of illegal liquor a dangerous but extremely profitable enterprise. For young Robert and a select group of others, this extracurricular activity was scary and exciting. The jingle in their pockets as they skated down King Street after school was exhiliarating.

Robert and his friends enjoyed fishing in the nearby creeks and waterways, sometimes pooling their 50 cent pieces to rent an old rickety wooden rowboat and row out into the St. Johns River in search of large-mouth bass. They would ride their bikes to the nearby bridges and fish with cane poles, long lines, and hooks, bringing home stringers of fish to fry for supper. With the Great Depression on, while they loved the sport of fishing, it was also serious business for hungry, growing boys.

Because of his penchant for reading, Robert was an above-average 8th Grade student at Landon Junior/Senior High School in 1930. He had a fascination for adventure books that focused on traveling the world and facing impossible challenges. Occasionally, he would get caught by his teachers with a novel by Earnest Hemingway or Herman Melville tucked in front of the textbook he was supposed to be studying.

When he wasn't scurrying around the woods late at night searching for firewood for old one-eye, Robert put his energies toward schooling and being with his friends. But his guard was always up ... he knew he was on his own and it was up to him to learn survival skills. Mama was busy, and Rut had his agenda of moonshining and money-making. If Robert wanted to make something of his life, that was his own business – nobody really cared one way or the other. He was determined to be somebody ... and always, there was that nagging knowledge that he was engaged in illegal activity.

Robert's 1930 Landon Yearbook shows that he was a member of the Up & Up Club, with its hopeful motto and the symbol of an airplane in flight.

Up and Up Club

The Up and Up Club has put its motto and its purpose into its name. It holds the City Championship for indoor flying, and has won three contests, scoring unusual success with indoor and outdoor flying and with scale models.

Commander-in-Chief—Otis Borum
Assistant Commander—Pulaski Broward

First Pilot—Linden Heston   Third Pilot—Sherwood Smith
Second Pilot—Warren Whitmore   Mechanic—Hoyt Broward

Sponsor—Miss Kathleen Turney

Cecil Butler   O. H. McKagen
Leland Coutant   Walter Nolan
Robert Dean   Allen Pearce
Arli Elomore   Bethune Phillips
Richard Empie   Jesse Ryon
Homer French   Robert Swindell
Henry Furman   Francis Williams
William Hall   Harold Jacquett
Edward Hudnall

52

Robert Lee Swindell (just before nine o'clock)

18

By the time he became a 9th grader at Landon, Robert's role as a moonshiner had increased considerably. Now, he knew how to brew the liquor and there were times when Rut wanted him to stand in for Old One-eye, who sometimes didn't show up after a long night of sampling "white lightning." There was a twofold reason for the liquor they produced to be called white lightning. First, the recipe for moonshine is simply corn meal, sugar, yeast and water, and all whiskey is clear (white) when it is first distilled. The whiskey that we now buy at the local liquor store has been aged for years in charred oak barrels, giving it an amber color and mellow taste. Moonshine (white lightning) had no aging requirements. It was bottled and sold straight from the still. The clear liquor that resulted had a kick that gave it the name "lightning."

With his quick mind and innate powers of observation, Robert had soon learned that making alcohol revolves around two processes: fermentation and distillation. Fermentation, a chemical reaction that occurs when yeast breaks down the sugar, results in alcohol. Distillation evaporates the alcohol at 172 degrees, collecting the steam before condensing it back into liquid form, thus the constant replenishing of firewood.

There was also the matter of those damn revenuers! It seemed like as soon as still really got up and running and started producing a regular income for Rut and his partners, they would hear that a raid was being planned and they'd have to move the still to another location. Robert would be enlisted to help clear the area and haul the equipment elsewhere. Locating another base of operations was no problem in Jacksonville back in those days ... thick wooded areas abounded, but it was still unsettling. Because he never actually came face to face with a revenuer, Robert considered the last-minute escapes just another adventure. He had that feeling of invincibility that comes with youth ... "Some boys would discover the still in the woods and then we'd quick move it before we got caught" he recalls. "Sometimes I wished I was just one of those boys wandering around in the woods, instead of one of the moonshiners leaving."

Low Ninth Grade

First Row: John Amos, Margaret Beasley, Junior Bowden, Willard Buie, Jimmie Brown, Ethel Bryant, John Cason, Mildred Collins, Leland Coutant.

Second Row: Winifred Cook, Alethea Cruz, Dorothy Dickinson, Richard Empie, Julius Eshe, William Fiore, Virgil Fiveash, Louise Gavagan.

Third Row: Clarafae Ginn, Clara Grinsted, Randolph Groom, George Haines, Calvin Hayden, Edward Hewitt, Frances Hudnall, Gladys Jackson.

Fourth Row: Willie Lankford, Marion Marjenhoff, J. T. McCormick, Marjorie Mier, Ernest Ortagus, Esther Osteen, Reba Oswald, Ben Parks, Russell Patten.

Fifth Row: Marguerite Ridge, Wilmoth Robarts, Leona Shaw, Betty Sisson, Frances Starratt, Charles Sparks, Jeff Sumerall, Robert Swindell, Millie Wilkinson.

Sadly, Robert's moonshining activities soon overshadowed his school work and when he was in 9th grade at Landon, he quit school.

The fact that his 1930 and 1931 Landon Yearbooks were still in his possession more than eight decades later is just one indication of the regret he still harbors about quitting school.

"I always regretted leaving school in 9th grade. I didn't have anybody to push me – to make me go to school. I made sure that didn't happen with my kids. I pushed them. They needed an education and they should have it. Seems like at one time after I stopped going to school, I thought about going back. I knew what was right and what was wrong. Quitting school was wrong. I had eyes and ears and I knew what the law allowed and what the law didn't allow."

Yes, he knew what the law allowed and what it didn't ... but he was 14 years old, making more money than most grown men ... and he was having fun! Every day he woke up wondering what the next adventure would be!

CHAPTER 3
PROOF!

"The revenuers had to have proof it was us. We'd haul ass and they'd never catch us!"

Now that he was free of school obligations, Robert could devote full-time to keeping ahead of the revenuers while learning all there was to know about moonshining.

"There was nothing to making moonshine," he remembers. "You set up the water and the 'buck' (cornmeal) – 50 pounds of sugar and 50 pounds of buck in the wooden barrel. It would start working (bubbling) – took about three days. Then it went through a funnel down little copper pipes and it turned from steam to liquid and then we caught it in five-gallon jugs. We sold it to the distributors and we were the distillery (that's why it's called a still)."

Once in a while, he admits, he would taste it just to see how it tasted. He never just drank it, even though he knew he could. It was just there, in volume, and he'd take a drink – maybe even two – but he never got drunk. "I don't care to get drunk," he says. "When you're drunk, you don't know what the hell you're doing. I always want to know what I'm doing."

Soon, Robert was involved in every aspect of the bootlegging business. He even helped make some of the copper pipes, buying sheet copper from a place in Jacksonville. Once the shine was caught in the five gallon jugs, they needed to be taken from the woods and stored elsewhere. Robert learned how to carry two five gallon jugs at once – one by hand and the other balanced on his shoulder.

One day Robert was asked to deliver a five-gallon jug to a designated spot on the side of the road next to some stay-wires running up an electrical pole. He was instructed to put it right out in the open in plain sight where somebody could come by and pick it up. He did what he was told. He knew they'd come get it, but it still felt strange to just plunk it down next to the road and walk away.

They usually transported the jugs of shine into town by car and stored them at a house until they were ready to be distributed to the buyers.

Most of the cars, as he remembers, were Fords ... fast Fords. In fact, there was a day when they were driving a Ford filled with five-gallon jugs and spotted the law closing in. Quickly turning onto a dirt road and racing through the woods up to the top of a hill in Arlington, Robert and Rut jumped out of the shine-loaded car and pushed it over the hill into a bluff. "We didn't throw the car away - just hid it close to the crossroads, with the river on one end and Atlantic Blvd. on the other. It was somewhere near where Jacksonville University is today," he muses, narrowing his eyes at the memory and grinning a mischievous grin.

Another time, Robert was delivering white lightning in the exclusive neighborhood of Avondale. He saw that the law was coming around the corner toward him and he jumped out of the car, ran across the street and through the front door of a house. The people appeared to be at home, but he didn't stop to chat ... he just ran through the house like "lightning" and out the back door, jumping the fence and running all the way through Confederate Park. He was out of breath when he stopped running and started walking casually in the neighborhood, coming up on a man in front of his house working in the yard. He asked the man for a lift home, and that was the end of that adventure. Robert never went back to get the moonshine, and he never knew the name of the people whose house he used as an escape route.

Robert and a buddy once were delivering some peach-flavored moonshine to Blackshear, Georgia. They were in Robert's hopped up Model-A Ford and made their delivery early in the day so that they could drop by and visit a couple of girls they'd met on the last run. Robert got to his girl's house and his buddy borrowed his car to go off to visit his girl across town. After a while, the fellow came back and was in a big hurry. "We gotta go!" he told Robert. "We gotta go right now!" Not one to question that kind of urgency, Robert jumped in the passenger side of his Model-A and they took off down the road. Pretty soon, the fellow told Robert, "We gotta stop!" Pulling the car into an old abandoned barn on the side of the road, they sat there in silence until Robert asked what was going on. "I hit a man's cow," his buddy confessed. Robert got out and looked at the Model-A on the driver's side and sure enough, the front was all crinkled and messed up. "Let's wait here until it gets good and dark," said his buddy. "I hit that man's cow and they're out looking for me. Sorry about your car. I'll pay for the damage when we get home." After dark, they drove back to Jacksonville in Robert's damaged car. He never saw that "buddy" again, and he never got paid for the damage done to his car.

Thankfully, Robert was making enough money selling white lightning that he could afford to repair a damaged fender, and much more. One night he was coming back from delivering shine to Jacksonville Beach in his Model-A Ford and he attracted an officer in a V8 Ford. This was way before consolidation in Jacksonville and the officer was a Duval County Road Patrol - all Robert had to do was beat him to the Jacksonville city limits and he'd be home-free because the patrol didn't have jurisdiction in the city. He hauled ass down Beach Boulevard (now Atlantic) and outran the patrol and when he got to the city limits, he stopped. The Duval County Road Patrol Officer knew he was beaten. He got out of his car and walked over to Robert. "I've got one question," he said. "I gotta look under the hood of that car because I couldn't keep up with you and I've got a brand new V8!"

Yes, the cars driven by the moonshiners were fast. They had to be! In fact, the souped up cars were necessary in order to give the slip to the federal tax agents determined to bust them. Runners like Robert built their reputations by outsmarting and outdriving the law ... and sometimes, they held informal races to prove one was faster than another. Eventually, those races became organized sport and by 1947, there was a meeting in Daytona Beach of drivers, car owners and mechanics (some of them former moonshiners), to establish racing rules. They formed the National Association for Stock Car Auto Racing (NASCAR) and the rest is history.

For one particular young moonshiner in the 1930's, having a hopped up Model-A made Robert able to "safely" deliver moonshine to points north and south of Jacksonville without getting caught by the revenuers. Robert knew that the law was always looking for cars that were jacked up or sagging in the back. If they were sagging, it meant that they were full of shine. If they were jacked up, it meant that the shine had been delivered. Either way, the law was prone to stopping suspicious looking cars. So, Robert figured out a way to fool the revenuers. He hired a garage in Jacksonville to put little "helper blocks" in the springs so that when he loaded his car for a delivery to Miami, the car would run level. Then, when he got to Miami and unloaded the car, he hired another garage there to take out the helper blocks so that the car, again, would run level. There was no doubt that young Robert Lee Swindell was one "level-headed" young moonshiner.

There was one time, though, when nothing he did on a moonshine run to Miami was any good at all. He was driving a rental car full of shine at the time, and was being chased so hard that he ran the car right off the road into a canal and was forced to abandon it ... shine and all.

Robert and his buddies had many close calls over the next few years, but there was only one time that he was actually arrested. "The law rounded up a bunch of us, but I never spent the night in jail. They knew we were moonshining, but they never actually walked in and saw us."

There were about a dozen young men lined up to go into a courtroom hearing. They were called in, one by one. "They called my name – Robert Lee Swindell – and I went up and sat at the table in front of the judge and jury. I told a lie and got out of it. Part of it was true." The Judge asked Robert if he was one of the boys making whiskey down at the beach, to which he answered, "No sir. I don't fool with that stuff." The Judge was incensed. "What do you mean? You were down there!" he said. Robert told him that he was working on the seawall off to one side – making bricks for the seawall. He explained that he was at a different spot than the other boys, curing bricks for the seawall by pouring water on them and keeping them moist. It just so happened that he was there at the same time as the others … he couldn't help that. The judge and jury believed him and let him go. There were three or four that went ahead of Robert – one by one – and several that followed.

Robert was the only one that got set free.

Possibly his believability stemmed from the part of his story that was, indeed, true. Not one to be idle, Robert had really been working on the seawall part of the time, wetting down the bricks and waiting for them to cure. He had walked up the beach to where a ditch was being dug to build the seawall and noticed that they were sinking concrete slabs into the beach. He knew the crane operator who was there every day digging the ditch and once in a while, Robert would crawl up into the crane and watch him operating it. It wasn't long before the crane operator asked Robert if he wanted to help drive it, which he did. "Every once in a while, I'd get a chance to make a lift. Pretty soon, I was driving the crane by myself!"

It also wasn't long before Robert realized that there was no future in moonshining and a decent, honest job like driving a crane began to look good to him. That close call in court, compounded with having to lie his way out of it, brought back some of the heroic, valiant lessons he'd learned while reading the old classics. Robert decided it was time to grow up. His moonshine days were over, but he had accumulated enough adventure stories to last a century ... or more!

CHAPTER 4
GLADYS

Eighteen years old and in pursuit of a real job, Robert was working the dredge at Olson's shipyard when he ran into another reason to set his sights on the straight and narrow ... her name was Eva Gladys Olson, age 17, and just about the prettiest girl he'd ever seen.

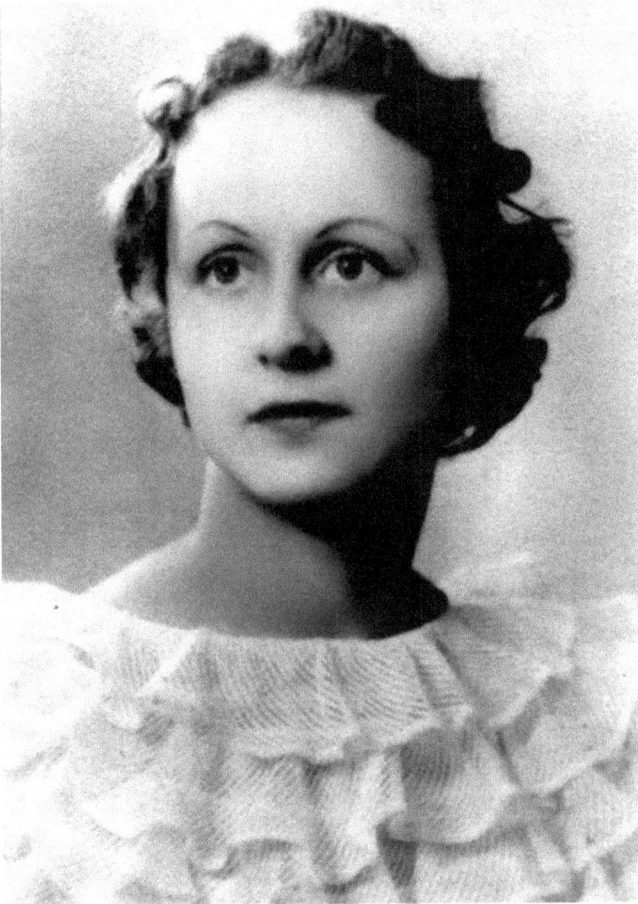

Eva Gladys Olson

On a fall day in 1935, Robert was driving near the main part of Arlington, where the Olson's had a big house. He noticed Gladys Olson right away. She was walking on the side of the road from the store to their house – about halfway in between – and carrying a heavy jug of water. He pulled up next to her – slow and easy, like, and said, "Get in. I'll give you a ride." She shook her head no. He said, "C'mon, it's just a little way. I'm not going to bother you," but she said, "No!" Robert drove off that day, but he didn't give up. "She was pretty," he recalls … "Prettier than me!"

Gladys was the daughter of Robert's boss, Bowen D. Olson, Sr., and his wife, Eva Smith Olson of J. Olson & Sons Shipyards. Eva Olson did not approve of "that boy and his bunch that hang out around the crossroads." She warned Gladys to be careful and not get involved with any of that bunch. When Halloween came, Robert and his bunch of friends painted their faces and got dressed up – and that just confirmed what Eva Olson suspected … they were a wild bunch! She really didn't know the half of it!

Robert saw Gladys every chance he got – courting her with gifts and gab. He did some work for Western Union, delivering telegrams that took him to Arlington and when he was in the neighborhood, he would stop by and see her. He took the ferry from downtown to Arlington and delivered telegrams on his bike. He once got a $20 tip for delivering a telegram to Arlington – a rare occurrence in those days when the nation was still recovering from the Great Depression. Sometimes, he would stop at Keys Chili Parlor downtown and get a tamale, saltine crackers and a bowl of chili for 15 cents.

By December of that same year, Gladys had decided that Robert was the man for her. He was handsome and exciting and funny and one of the best dancers she'd ever danced with.

Gladys had met the love of her life and it didn't matter how her parents felt about him. She was going to marry this man, come hell or high water! They eloped on Christmas Eve, going to a Justice of the Peace in MacClenny. By the time they got there, the Justice and his wife had already turned in for the night, so they woke them up. While they were waiting, another eager couple drove up. Robert and Gladys went in the house and were married first, with the other couple standing up for them, and then they stood up for the other couple. It turned out that both young couples were from Jacksonville.

So, now Robert was a married man and had a wife to come home to. He knew his moonshining days were really over.

Oddly enough, although the 21st Amendment to the Constitution had repealed Prohibition in 1933 (two years before they got married), the new laws left the matter of Prohibition up to state governments. Bootleggers continued to make a profit on the sale of illegal liquor because several states, including Alabama, Arkansas, Florida, Kansas, Kentucky, Mississippi, Texas and Virginia, had high concentrations of dry counties then, and still do to this day.

In this year of 2017, there continue to be moonshiners and bootleggers and makers of white lightning, especially in the hills of West Virginia, where thousands of gallons of illicit whiskey still pour from the backwoods. There is even a series now called "Moonshiners" on the Discovery Channel, and the stigma that was attached to that activity back in the 1930's and 40's is no longer. It's almost in style today, but it certainly was not in style then, especially for the church-going crowd in Arlington, of which Eva Olson was a leader.

Gladys's Dad, Bowen David Olson, was adamant that she could not marry a moonshiner – and he had heard about Robert's activities – but once they were married, Olson grudgingly saw that Robert was a determined young man and a hard worker who loved their daughter and would do his best to take good care of her. At first, when Robert's mother, Eva, heard that he had gotten married, she told him she didn't care for Gladys, but that didn't bother Robert at all. His mother had never been around much anyway.

The Olson's, on the other hand, were very much in evidence – both at work and at home.

Robert and Gladys moved into a small house in Arlington, within sight of the Olson's big house. Robert's sister, Mildred, had married Gladys's brother, B. D. Olson, Jr., by then, and they lived in a house not far from the big house. Their marriage didn't last, and Mildred, who was a beautiful girl, was destined to marry twice before she died of heart problems at the young age of 38.

Even though Robert worked with Olson Shipyards and Gladys was a member of the family, the young couple was too proud to ask for help one Christmas when they were so impoverished they couldn't pay their electricity bill. So, to make extra money, Robert would pull moss out of the trees to sell to the mattress factory downtown. After taking out the back seat of his car and filling it with moss, he would hunt squirrels for dinner. He taught Gladys how to make squirrel gravy. By then, he had learned to shoot only in the head, so it didn't destroy any of the squirrel meat.

Those were hard times, but they were temporary. Forever after, they would remember that sad dark Christmas when they sat looking up at the Christmas lights twinkling in the Olson houses.

Bobby

It wasn't long before things started looking up for the Swindell family with the birth of their first son, Robert (Bobby) Lee Swindell, Jr. on the 18th of May, 1938. When Robert held his newborn son for the first time, all he could think of was, "Now I have to get my act straightened out! There goes the bullshit!" It was an epiphany for him. He was a father now and that responsibility was heavy on his shoulders, especially as he had lost his father at such an early age and had endured such a lack of parenting from his mother. Robert was determined not to let his kids get into trouble, especially with moonshine! He was going to make sure they didn't quit school like he had and that they got a good education. No one had ever pushed him to excel, but he most certainly was planning to push his kids just as hard as he could push them.

In the meantime, while Gladys took care of Bobby in their tiny house, Robert started operating the huge crane – maintaining the docks at the shipyards. He was one of the few crane operators who knew what he was doing, and he never had an accident with a crane. "Nobody really taught me how to drive a crane," he says, "but I taught quite a few."

In anticipation of World War II, Robert went to work out at Camp Blanding moving sand to the beach to get the training area ready for construction. When he got a call from the Colonel of the Army Corps of Engineers requesting that he train some engineers on using heavy equipment – link-belt cranes, bulldozers, etc., he asked, "Why me? The other guy has seniority. Why don't you ask him to do the training?" The Colonel's answer was puzzling. "He doesn't have the temperament to do this job."

As it turned out, the engineers Robert was being asked to train were an all-black engineering unit. He did, after all, have the temperament to train these particular engineers quickly and quietly and then turn the job over to them. For some reason, possibly because he was so well-read and such a deep-thinker, he lacked many of the prejudices that were rampant in the Old South at that time in history.

"Hell, I'd worked around black people - green or black or white – I wasn't worried about where you come from or what you look like – just do the work right!" Robert helped a great many engineers learn how to operate the crane. He took them under his wing gladly.

When World War II finally came along, Robert tried to enlist twice in the military but was considered too valuable at home. It made him angry. "During the war, all the damn cranes were needed and I ended up in charge. I rode some cranes and then I'd get operators for them. I'd put one man up on a crane as it came in, show him how the machine worked and tell him to follow the directions of the flag man. I trained one and then another and all of a sudden, it was a flood. There were lots of different cranes, but all of them operated the same way once you got past the make of them."

Operating the cranes at Camp Blanding and at Olson's Shipyards kept Robert busy, while Gladys and their little boy, Bobby, spent a good deal of time with her mother, Eva, doing work through the church for the war effort.

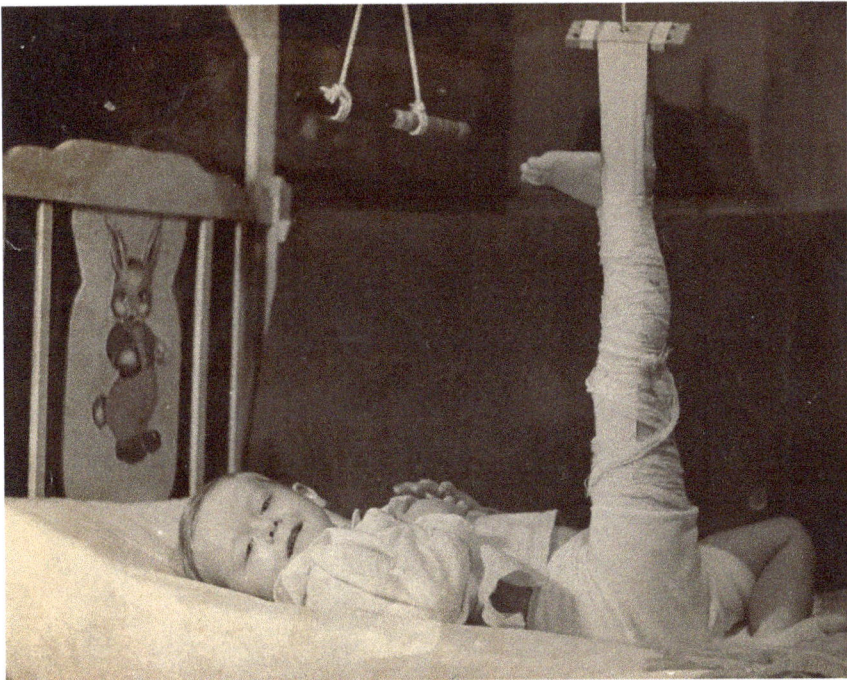

When Bobby was about 3 years old, he broke his leg and it had to be put into a sling suspended in the air. There just wasn't room for that kind of set-up in the tiny Swindell house, so Bobby stayed with his Grandma Eva while his leg was in the cast.

Grandma Eva was a devout Methodist who received a visit from her pastor nearly every day. Having the boy in such a captive position was just too good an opportunity for his mischievous Uncles, B. D. and Leslie Olson, to pass up. Whenever they had the chance, they would sneak in and pump the little boy full of cuss words and make suggestions about how

Robert & Bobby Swindell

he could best use them. One day, as the pastor was approaching the open front door, poor innocent little Bobby yelled out, "Eva, that damn preacher's here again!"

But despite his pesky uncles, Bobby Swindell was the hope for the future in his father's eyes – Robert wanted him to have everything that he had missed as a boy – especially the guidance and discipline needed to succeed. A handsome man, Robert was proud of his equally handsome son, Bobby. Bobby was about four years old and Gladys was expecting a second child when they moved into a larger house nearby, and even started buying new living room furniture.

Robert's second son, William Henry (Billy) Swindell (named after his Uncle Henry – Robert David's brother), was born on December 14, 1942. Gladys doted on Billy because he was so beautiful. She simply could not talk herself into getting his pretty blonde hair cut and poor big brother, Bobby, had to put up with a great deal of teasing from the neighborhood kids about his pretty little brother!

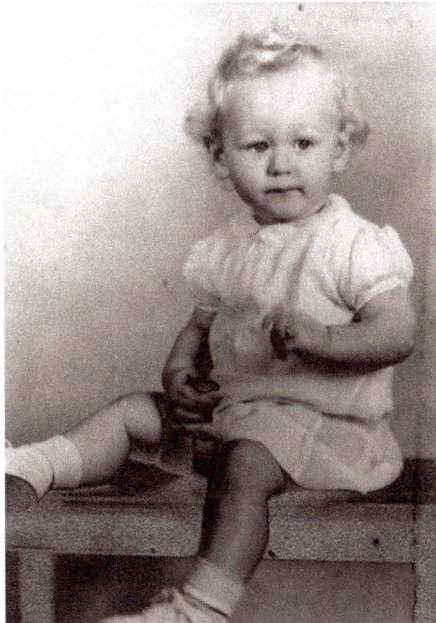

Billy Swindell

45

Billy was about 2½ years old when a storm blew the roof off of the little house near Arlington. Robert was at the shipyards when the storm hit and Gladys walked with her two little boys through the pounding rain and wind to a cinderblock barbershop nearby – the most secure place to weather the storm. Afterward, when she discovered that the roof was gone and all of her brand new living room furniture had been destroyed, Gladys was absolutely furious. She put Billy and Bobby in the 1940 Dodge that was in the driveway and drove directly to the house at 1106 Bee Street. "I found a house," she told Robert when she went to pick him up at work. "I want to move." And that is exactly what they did.

**Robert and Gladys raised their kids
in this house at 1106 Bee Street**

The Swindell family lived in that two-bedroom, one bath house for many years. "We grew up in the house on Bee Street," recalls Billy. "We were not wealthy, but we were never hungry. Dad worked. Mom raised the children. There were French doors out to the porch where I slept and Dad planted Spanish Bayonet underneath the windows (probably to keep Bobby from climbing out). Dad also built a brick barbecue pit where family and friends enjoyed many cookouts and oyster roasts. We would move furniture out of the living room on Friday nights for parties and dancing. There are many good memories associated with the house on Bee Street."

Fishing was a big part of the family time Robert spent with his sons. They fished at Plumbers Cove, on the Intracoastal Waterway, at the Jetties and St. Johns River and many of the creeks and canals nearby. Gladys would fix a hearty breakfast for Robert and the boys at about 4:00 a.m. so that they could go to the beach and catch bait. Then, often, they'd go to Epping Forest or Christopher Creek to fish, bringing sardines in mustard or barbecue sauce, saltine crackers and Vienna sausages, and Robert's home-made brew. Inevitably, they'd come home with a nice catch – pose for a picture if the fish were big enough, and then get to cleaning the fish so Gladys could fry them up for supper.

Bobby and Bill – Big Bass

Then there was the day when Bobby and his dad were fishing off of Epping Forest. They'd gotten up at 4 a.m. and driven to the Intracoastal Waterway to catch bait and then come back to rent one of the old leaky wooden boats at Goodbye's Lake. Robert attached his "Kicker" (10-15 horsepower motor) to take them out to his favorite fishing spot.   Sometimes it would take 30 to 45 minutes for him to get to the perfect fishing spot, trolling so long that whichever of the kids was with him would fall asleep.

That day, when his drowsy son opened his eyes, he saw that his dad wasn't catching any fish. "I don't think my spore is right," Robert said, taking a big swig of home-brew. Soon after he took a drink, he caught a fish.   He took another drink and caught another fish. It was a method that worked and he kept doing it - catching many fish that day. When they finally pulled up to shore, Robert said to Bobby, "You tie it up. I'll get the kicker." Unsteady ... for some reason ... he reached for the kicker and fell headfirst overboard. Bobby was treated to some colorful language as his dad emerged in waist-deep water still holding that kicker.

Bobby has always said that if the water had been 100 feet deep, his dad would have drowned, because he wasn't going to let go of that kicker for anything.

Bobby was about 12 years old when he caught a big bass that looked like a winner for the Finklestein's Sporting Goods Fishing Contest. Robert and Bobby took the fish down to the Bay Street store where it was weighed and a photo was taken of the young fisherman. As was the custom, the judges cut a hole in the stomach of the fish to make

Bobby's Big Bass!

sure it hadn't been weighted down with sinkers. Sure enough, the 12-pound bass was a winner!

Gladys, Darlene and Bobby

Bobby won a rod and reel for the biggest fish ... as he remembers, his Dad kept the rod and reel ... but they took the fish home and Gladys fried it up for supper! "We always ate what we caught, no matter what," remembers Bobby.

The big bass wasn't the best catch for Bobby that year that he turned 12, though ... not by a longshot! His adored baby sister, Ellen Darlene, was born on July 29, 1950, and having a pretty little girl around made the house on Bee Street buzz with excitement! Darlene was her Daddy's heart. Robert was smitten with her from the moment she was born, and her brothers adored her, too.

Now, Gladys finally had her little daughter to dress up and pamper, and although she liked pink frilly dresses for special occasions, Darlene was destined to be her father's daughter – a girl who loved to fish!

Easter Finery

One morning about 5 a.m. Robert came in and woke Darlene up. "Let's go fishing, girl," he told his 8-year old daughter, who was thrilled at the prospect of spending a day on the water with her dad. He sat her down in a little wooden boat and instructed

Darlene, Robert, Gladys and Billy

her to wait there while he walked over to Christopher's to get bait. Unfortunately, he had forgotten to put in the plug and the boat began to fill up with water. "Dad?" yelled Darlene, trying to get his attention while he was talking to someone at Christopher's. "Not now!" he yelled back, and went on talking. "But ... Dad!" Again he responded, "Not Now!!!" "Dad!" she finally shouted. "The boat's sinking!" Using some colorful language, Robert stomped back down the dock and let Darlene know that she was not in danger of drowning. "Have you ever been in a rowboat?" Robert asks, looking back at that day his daughter has always remembered with such terror. "I knew it wasn't going to sink right away."

Finally, when Darlene was about 11 or 12, she got old enough to really know how to fish, Swindell-style. "Dad was known to fish until you ran out of bait or beer, whichever came first," she recalls. "The rule was that you could not have your first beer until you caught your first fish, so I became really good at catching fish!" The beer, of course, was usually not store-bought, but homemade brew, and as always, with the beer, they took saltine crackers, Vienna sausage and sardines canned in mustard or barbecue sauce.

Now that their family was complete, Robert and Gladys settled into a routine that included strict discipline and strong guidance, melded with a great deal of love and laughter. The Swindell family had many more memories to make together at the house on Bee Street as Robert's sons and daughter aimed at achievements that he had only been able to dream about when he was their age.

CHAPTER 5
UP and UP

When Robert joined the Up & Up Club as a Landon 8th Grader, he had no idea that he would be spending a large portion of his life high up in air operating cranes. No one taught him how to operate a crane ... he just watched and learned and became the best crane operator in Jacksonville. Becoming an expert at whatever he did was a habit for Robert.

Best Crane Operator – Robert Swindell

Yes, the Up & Up Club at Landon was, ironically, a foreshadowing of what was to come for Robert Lee Swindell. Now, as his wife and three children looked up to him for nurture and support, Robert moved on up in the world, becoming a 32nd degree Mason. In 1945, he was Senior Steward of the Duval Lodge and

Robert and Gary Thigpen

was destined to be a Mason for more than 75 years, mentoring many young men along the way. He brought both of his sons into the Masons and Bobby was Worshipful Master of Solomon Lodge No. 20 at 21 East First Street in Jacksonville in 2000. Robert's honorary title is Ambassador for the Shrine … a leader among men who has helped myriad others climb up the ladder of the Masons and then the Shriners.

A long-time friend of Robert's and the family, Gary Thigpen helped Darlene with the move when Robert bought the house in Satsuma. They were cleaning out a shed and Gary found a metal bucket with about three handfuls of rocks in it. "Robert, this doesn't have to go, does it?" Gary asked, suggesting that it could be thrown in the trash since it was just a few rocks. "No!" Robert responded. "You can't throw that away. I may need those rocks someday." Gary and Darlene still grin about that one, but in spite of his friend's unusual rock collection, Gary Thigpen was proud to give Robert Lee Swindell the well-deserved honorary title of Ambassador of the Shrine.

**Both Gladys and Mildred were members
of the Order of the Eastern Star**

In addition to involving his family and mentoring other men in the Masons, Robert devoted a great deal of time to teaching engineers how to do their jobs; captaining tugboats through rough waters; and always, always looking out for those who depended on him, whether they were crews, coworkers, friends or family.

He worked at three shipyards – St. Johns, Gibbs and Merrill-Stevens, running tugboats for Olson Marine Corp., owned by the family of his father-in-law, Bowen David Olson.

Olson named his tugboats after his sisters, Eva, Margaret, Thelma, Agnes and Ruth. Jobwise, Robert's areas of expertise became increasingly diverse and what he did was consistently done to the highest standard.

There was a single big splash, a diminishing series of waves, and the Navy tug ST 1978 was water-borne at the Olson Boatyards on Lake Beresford yesterday in the launching of the first of ten similar tugs to be built there. The tug is shown above just as she hit the water. (Heley Studio photo).

One of the tugboats Robert helped build during WWII

As noted, Robert was so skilled at operating the big cranes that he was kept building big liberty ships and training engineers rather than being allowed to enlist in the military service during WWII.

Looking back over the years, it seems that Robert left his footprint throughout the City of Jacksonville ... from the beaches and buildings at Camp Blanding to the piers at the Naval Air Station, to the bulkheads at Atlantic Beach to the foundations for the Main Street Bridge ... when one is up in the air over North Florida, there is evidence everywhere below that Robert Lee Swindell was here.

Robert was even on the job when he taught Bobby and Billy to swim between big piles of sand dredged up from Daytona to New Smyrna Beaches on the Indian River. He would tie a rope around their waists and pull them along, swimming back and forth with them until they learned to swim on their own. This was during the time that one of Robert's jobs was laying telephone and electrical cable across the Indian River – part of the Intracoastal waterway – from Daytona to Daytona Beach and New Smyrna. Robert would take his little family with him to this job and they would stay in a motel right there at New Smyrna Beach. In fact, Gladys learned to dog-paddle on the Indian River right along with her sons. Having grown up in a family that made their living on the water, she had, amazingly, never learned to swim.

"Robert is part of our family legend ... he was always amazing in his ability to learn and perform," recalled David Larry.

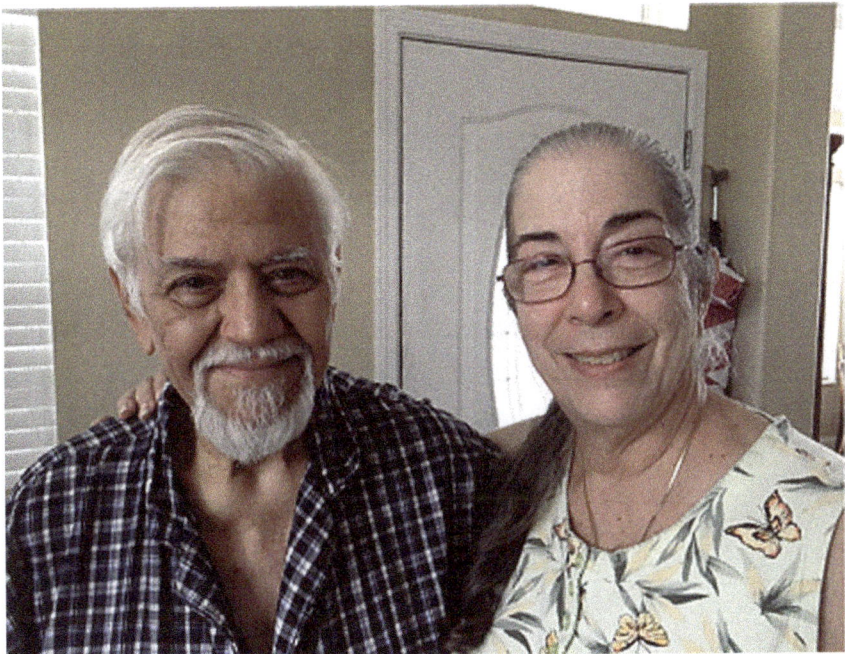

David & Sharon Larry of St. Augustine, Florida, contributed to this book

A cousin of Gladys's and grandson of Julius Olson, who founded the Olson Shipyards, David said, "Robert was the go-to guy. He had such a deft touch in controlling cranes that he was known as one of the best. It was the same way with tugboats ... when Robert captained a tug, the job would get done. He was one of the best on the river."

David, whose mother Thelma was an aunt of Gladys, says that his parents (Wilbur and Thelma) were close friends of Robert and Gladys. David has always looked up to Robert Swindell because he was a fine man who worked hard and earned respect. He is thankful that a book is finally being written about such a man.

David loves telling tales about Robert's escapades as a Tugboat Captain for Olson Marine, like the one about hauling an oversized barge through a narrow South Florida Canal. "By the time they knew the barge was too wide to fit through, it was already committed," recalls David. "There was no turning back." Somehow, with patience and ingenuity, Robert maneuvered the barge through the narrow passageway without causing any damage at all. Not so, David noted, with the string of three or four barges Robert's tugboat was hauling at St. Augustine. When one of the barges broke loose, due to some sort of tidal surge, it crashed into the Bridge of Lions and did quite a bit of damage. It was one of the few times when the tide won out over Robert's determination.

David's parents knew Robert before he and Gladys got married. They talked of what a "ladies man" Robert was when he was a young moonshiner, and what a great dancer. Many years later, Robert regaled young David Larry with stories about his moonshine days, telling him secrets of the trade such as the fact that they used Blackjack oak (scrub oak) for their fires when possible because it didn't make a lot of smoke and, therefore, the revenuers had less chance of spotting the still in the woods. Robert talked of the necessity to be in good shape because he had often been required to haul 100 pound bags of sugar and grain through dense woods.

"He told me repeatedly that there was nothing glamorous about moonshining ... it was pure hard work," said David. One story of Robert's that stuck in David's memory was the location of the still in Arlington – so close to the homes in that area – and how, when the moonshiners had to leave that particular still in a hurry, they put the dregs from the bottom of the barrel into one big jug. They took that jug to North Carolina and people there thought it was the best moonshine they'd ever tasted.

They sold the moonshine dregs from the Arlington still to people in North Carolina for four times what they were getting for white lightning in Jacksonville.

David Larry was six years old when Bobby Swindell was born and he remembers going to Bee Street with his parents and visiting. The two young couples would often break open a bottle and play rummy – an inexpensive and enjoyable pastime during those depression years.

"They all loved to dance and they spent a lot of time together – even lived in the same house a few times," recalls David. Even though she was a contemporary of his mother's, Gladys was David Larry's favorite cousin. She was open and frank with people, "knew all the secrets of all the church-goers in Arlington, and didn't mind sharing them, either." Everyone who was anyone in Arlington attended the United Methodist Church, David remembers, and he, along with Bobby and Billy Swindell, was part of the Methodist Youth Fellowship.

David nicknamed his favorite cousin "Gladiola." He smiles when he remembers how much fun Gladys was and how she loved to dance. When he went over to England with the U.S. Air Force and became engaged to an English girl named Dee, he brought her back to Jacksonville and they were married in his cousin's house on Bee Street. "That house on Bee Street where Robert and Gladys raised their children was a good place," he says. "I loved going back to it."

David's fiancé, Dee, stayed with the Swindell family for about a week prior to their marriage and, as she was an English girl who had only used public transportation and didn't know how to drive, Gladys decided to do her a favor and teach her. It was 1955 and the Swindell's had a brand new 1954 Plymouth. Dee got behind the wheel and backed out of the driveway so fast that she sped into the park across the street and scraped the side of the car on a Stop Sign. Gladys, being the smart, wily lady she was, made sure she parked the car so that Robert wouldn't see the damage when she went to pick him up at work.

Luckily (or not), Bobby begged to pick his dad up at work about a week later and, because he didn't yet have a driver's license, Gladys told him to take the back roads. He would have been fine except that a Mayport sailor, who was unfamiliar with the roads in Jacksonville and driving the wrong way on a one-way street, ran into Bobby at the same time that Bobby was running a stop sign, and rolled the Plymouth, causing a great deal more damage than the scrape Dee had incurred. Bobby was not injured and even more shocking, his dad did not punish him for getting in the accident. Actually, the accident made the local newspaper, with a headline that read: *"In Algebra, two minuses make a plus. Not so, when two vehicles each make a mistake."*

As far as Dee's incident, Gladys only told Robert about that after the new Plymouth got repaired.

In remembering their wedding at the Bee Street house, David Larry also recalled that Robert's beautiful sister, Mildred, arranged flowers for the special day and served tea.

Mildred

"Mildred was elegant and beautiful," he said, adding that both she and her first husband, his cousin, B.D., died much too young.

When Gladys gave birth to Darlene, she was so pretty that everyone said she resembled her Aunt Mildred, and sure enough, as she got older, the resemblance became more and more noticeable.

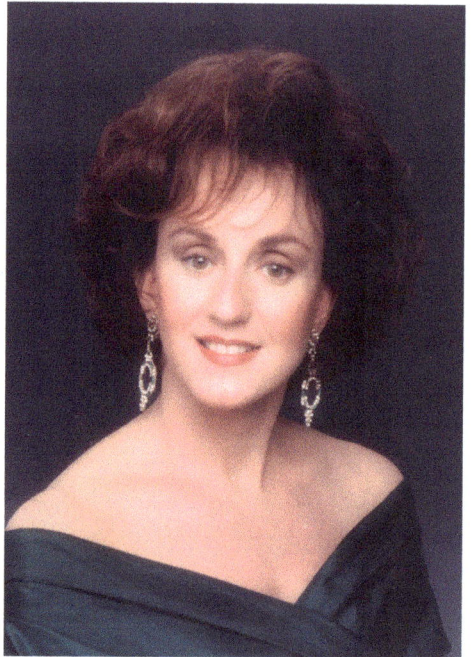

Darlene

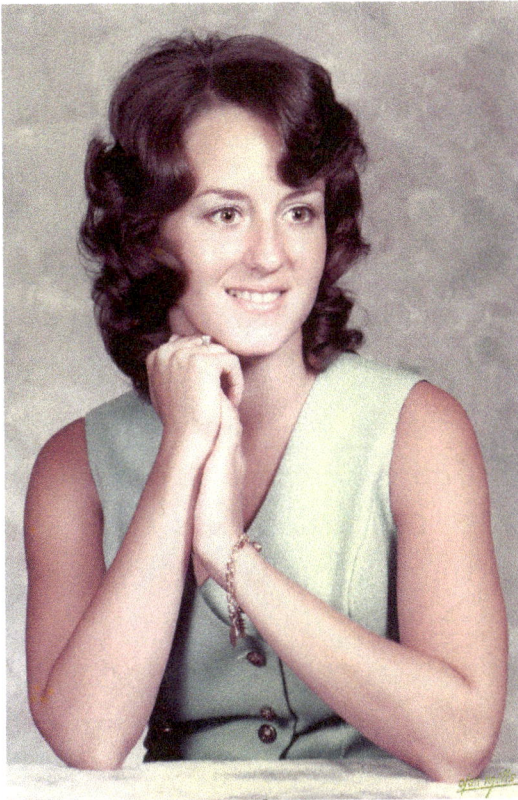

Darlene

Darlene was only about 8 years old when her Aunt Mildred died at age 38. "She had heart problems of some sort - I've heard it was an enlarged heart," says Darlene. "Today, she probably wouldn't have died – the doctors could fix it, but not back then." She remembers walking into her aunt's expensive apartment in downtown Jacksonville and being awed because it was all white. "Back in the 1950's, an all-white décor was really something special.

Aunt Mildred was married to a very wealthy man named John Mondello, who treated her like a queen."

John and Mildred adopted a little girl named Carol and had what seemed to be a charmed life until things started to fall apart. First, John Mondello died, and within a short time, Mildred also passed away. At the time that Mildred died, Carol was about five or six years old. Her maternal grandmother, Eva, took over raising the little girl. Yes, this was the same Eva who had been too busy working to pay attention to her own children, Robert and Mildred. Eva had married Clarence Hinson afer becoming widowed for the second time when Rut Aderhold was killed in a car accident on Kings Avenue running moonshine. It was another irony of life that the lady who had twice been widowed as a result of moonshine-related deaths, and had neglected her own children to make ends meet, was now responsible for raising her adopted granddaughter.

CHAPTER 6
HOME BREW AT BEE STREET

While life at the Swindell house on Bee Street wasn't exactly privileged like that of Aunt Mildred and Uncle John had been, the family lacked for nothing – Robert made sure of that. One thing that was always available was the home brew that Robert made out in the woodshed. After all, if anyone knew how to make it, he did. There was no reason for him to have to buy beer for fishing trips – he always had some brew on hand. As the boys grew, they learned to help their Dad out in his home brewery by forming an assembly line with the final product being stored in 5-gallon glass jugs. He taught them that the "cookings" at the top would indicate when it was aged properly and ready to be sucked up through a hose and placed in a bottle. They filled about five jugs at a time to be stored for use when needed. Friends knew they could get some good home brew from Robert Swindell. He didn't sell it ... he gave it away.

To this day, Bobby Swindell and his wife, Barbara, remember that home brewery with a shudder. "I was dating Barbara and she came over to the house to see me," says Bobby. "Dad and I were out fishing when she got there and Billy decided he would take her out to the garage and show her how to suck up the home brew through the hose and put it in the bottle. He didn't tell her not to swallow it. When we got home, I asked where Barbara was and Billy just said, 'She's inside.' She was inside alright! She was on the couch 'three sheets to the wind,' and Mother was really mad! I took her home and pushed her through the front door and ran. When I called later that day, her mother said she had a terrible case of the flu – she was sick as a dog. Barbara and I have been married for 57 years and she has never forgotten what Billy did to her … but she loves him anyway."

Then there was that hot summer day when Robert and Gladys were entertaining some friends in the living room of the little house at Bee Street and suddenly, it sounded like fireworks were going off right next to them. Pow! Pow! Pow! They had stored a few jugs of home brew in a closet and the heat had gotten to them. Lesson learned: Never store home brew in an enclosed place where it gets hot!

Growing up in the Swindell household, there were many lessons to be learned – some harder than others. Bobby was a teenager, eager to have a vehicle to drive, so he was excited when his dad hauled home a flatbed truck that wouldn't start and told him if he could fix it, he could drive it. Bobby took the engine completely apart – alternator, starter, everything – and then took all of the parts to Pagonis' Car Shop on Atlantic Blvd. and Kings Avenue. "Those were the days when families knew families," Bobby recalls, "and Mr. Pagonis was happy to test every part for me. He declared each part in good shape, but when I put it all back together, the truck still wouldn't start."

He was going to work more on it, but a little time went by and one day he came home and the truck was gone. Robert had traded it for a dog and couple of fishing rods. When Bobby complained, Robert told him, "You did well, but you didn't do the whole job." He explained to Bobby that the truck had a firing system and all he would have had to do was plug in the wires, because everything else on the truck was in good shape. "I don't know if

Mr. Pagonis didn't think about telling me or if I was supposed to ask him," says Bobby, "but I learned a lesson."

Bobby and Darlene

Robert was a disciplinarian. He rarely had to say anything twice. Kids were to speak only when spoken to ... to be seen and not heard. When Robert whistled for the kids to come home for supper, they knew to come running! The sound of Dad's belt popping was not a good sound! And, it wasn't easy to get his attention when he was busy. Today, when Bobby and Billy look back at those growing up years, they laugh about the similarity their lives had to an old Bill Cosby skit ... when their dad was busy and didn't want to be disturbed, they would often hear a blast: "Jesus Christ, Billy! Dammit, Bobby!"

One rule that Robert insisted his children learn was not to mess with other peoples' stuff ... no matter what. Always ask before you touch something. Be careful not to mess with something that doesn't belong to you. Bobby came in from playing one day when he was about ten years old and ran to the refrigerator, opened the door, and found a MilKay Orange Drink bottle filled with clear liquid that looked like water. He was thirsty and took the cork out of the bottle and took a good healthy swig of what he thought was cold water. It was white lightning.

"When I realized it was burning a hole in me, I ran to the sink and poured the rest of the bottle out. When dad got home, he looked in the refrigerator and asked where that bottle was. I told him the water in it had tasted really bad, so I poured it out. He laid me across the bed and wore my butt out! It definitely did not belong to me!"

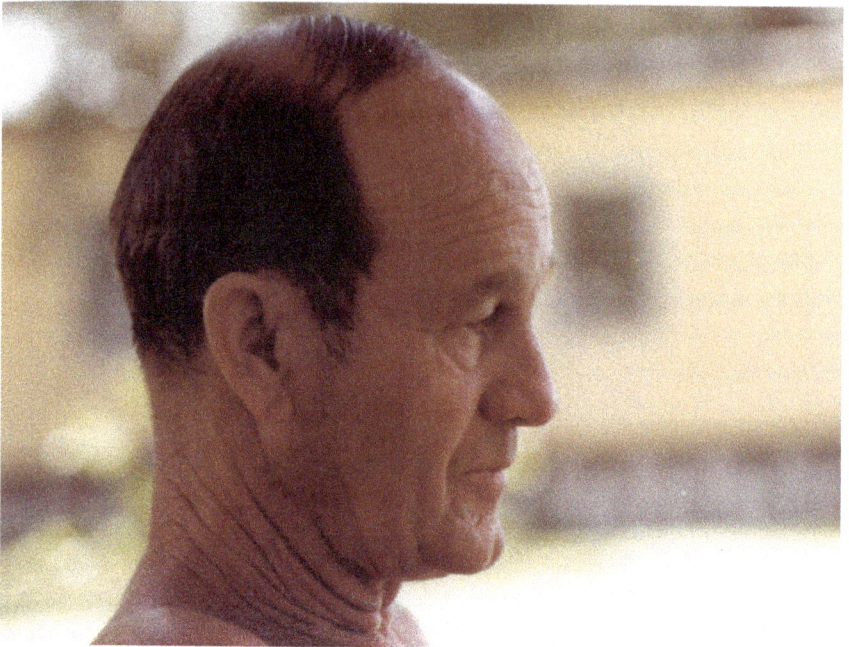

Robert

One day Darlene hesitantly said, "Dad?" Robert grimaced. "Not now!" "But, Dad…" "I told you, he growled. "Not Now!" Finally, she could hold it in no longer. "DAD, the tops are popping off your bottles in the garage!!" The odor that came from the garage when Darlene finally got her father's attention was sickening, to say the least.   It finally got to the point where home-brew and all of the accompanying "inconveniences" led to some actual trips to the grocery store to buy beer.

The house on Bee Street was right across the street from Marjenhoff Park (on the corner of Bee and Southampton). The Swindell kids played at the park nearly every day and when Robert got home from work, he would often cook dinner. As noted, when Robert whistled for the kids to come for dinner, he only did it once. If they didn't come, they were in big trouble. One night, Darlene ignored his whistle and when she got home, he had her cut her own switch from the tree at the corner of the house. He switched her legs and she didn't come home late again. There were a couple of other times that he had her cut her own switch from that tree and Darlene has often vowed that one day she'll go back to the house on Bee Street and cut down that tree.

There was a dump about three blocks away where Bee Street dead-ended and Darlene remembers being about 6 or 7 years old and running away to the dump. She was mad at Gladys and wanted to teach her a lesson, but when her mother caught up with her, it was the first and last time that Gladys ever spanked Darlene.

"We were the type of children who minded," Darlene recalls. "When you did something – you got punished and you never did it again. Bobby was the only one who did a few things more than once. He had a fascination for lizards and frogs and when he brought them home, Mother would lock him out of the house. He'd have the neighbor call and ask Mother if Bobby could come home for dinner now."

Robert was constantly bringing animals home and the children loved their pets. Darlene had asthma and Robert heard an old wives' tale that Chihuahuas were good for asthma, so he brought home Chico, the Chihuahua. Soon after Chico came to live there, Darlene went with her grandparents, Eva and Bowen, to the cemetery to clean headstones (as they did just about every other week). She begged to take Chico even though her grandfather insisted she would probably start playing and forget the dog. Sure enough, Granddad tied the little dog's leash to the bumper of the car and when it was time to go, they hopped in the car and drove off. "Where's your dog?" Grandpa asked, after they had driven slowly through the cemetery for a few minutes. Although they were only driving about five miles an hour, by the time they stopped and retrieved Chico, the poor little Chihuahua was definitely winded!

Gladys was good about Robert bringing home animals, with the exception of certain types that she could not tolerate. There was the time, for instance, when she was cleaning out Robert's lunchbox, that she found an unpleasant surprise. She had packed his lunch, as she did every day, in his big lunchbox that had two clips with a place for the thermos. Tied to one of the clips with a string that day was a huge bullfrog that Robert had found at the shipyard. When the frog leapt out at her, Gladys screamed her head off, set the lunchbox back on the counter and went after Robert, who sidestepped her and got out of the kitchen, quick! It took quite a while for her to get over being mad at Robert for that one, but eventually, he sweet-talked her into dancing with him again.

Dancing was something that everyone in the

Swindell family did often and with grace and precision. Bobby learned to dance in their living room at Bee Street and says that it served him well throughout high school and college. Few boys knew how to dance back then and he attributes his popularity to being able to "cut a rug" with the girls. It was one of the things that attracted Barbara to him. She often tells people that she dated another boy at one time, but he never danced. Bobby danced. He danced so well that he won her heart.

Dancing in their living room on Friday nights was a regular pastime for Robert and Gladys, and they loved it when the kids joined them.

Another inexpensive and enjoyable pursuit was going as a family to the drive-in movie at the corner of University and Atlantic Blvd. Robert crafted a wooden box for Billy to sit on in the back seat of their old 1940 Dodge, so that he could see the movies. Eventually, as the night wore on, Billy would crawl into the back window of that big car and fall asleep. Bobby remembers being old enough to sit outside the car on the ground and run to the concession stand for popcorn. The movie couldn't start until the sun went down, and in the summertime, that wasn't until nearly 8 p.m., so the kids would be treated to several cartoons and then it would be the previews of coming attractions and then the main feature.

Almost everything on the big screen in those days was in black and white. Robert and Gladys loved movies like "The Big Sleep," with Humphrey Bogart and "On the Town" with Fred Astaire and Ginger Rogers. Bobby remembers watching "A Star is Born" with Judy Garland, and, once in a great while, there would be an animated Disney Film in color. Snow White was Bobby's favorite. Sometimes on the weekend, there would be a double feature that lasted until well past midnight. Both boys would be fast asleep in the back of the big Dodge when they got home to Bee Street and Robert would pick up Billy, put Bobby over his shoulder, and take them to bed without either of them waking up until the next morning.

They had a square kitchen table and ate as a family. It was not a large kitchen, but many memorable events happened there. One night, Billy watched his Dad, after a night of celebrating, arm wrestle a man named Levene Jernigan. "That was the meanest looking man that I or any of my friends had ever seen," Billy remembers. "He was over 6'2", and weighed at least 250 pounds. When Dad put him down, he lost his balance and fell against our refrigerator, knocking it at least two feet across the floor. It was then that I realized just how strong a 5'8" man could be if he worked hard all his life."

And, despite his dad's well-known temper, Billy remembers that he kept his cool when he found out that he had been arrested and locked up in jail. Billy had called Bobby to bail him out, but the next day, a rookie officer called

Robert to apologize for locking Billy up. That was how Robert found out about it, since Billy had been spending the night with a friend and hadn't been missed. "The rookie locked me up because I didn't have my driver's license with me, but because I was 17, there was no record of my being jailed. It was destroyed."

Back at the Swindell kitchen, Gladys usually reigned, unless Robert was doing the cooking. She had not cooked much as a girl because she was left-handed, and for some reason, her mother didn't think she could learn to cook with that "handicap," but by the time the boys came along, she was cooking great meals for her family. One of her main teachers was, of course, Robert. As always, when he learned to do something – anything – he did it well, and he had been cooking since he was a boy watching his Grandma Janie cook beans. Robert also did a lot of the cooking for the family simply because he enjoyed it, having become an expert cook on the tugboats and in the backyard. Once in a while, he'd take the kids out on a tugboat, and cook for them on the open water. Those were rare, but happy, times on the tugboats for Robert ... not stressful, as so many of the tugboat captaining jobs turned out to be.

Billy remembers that at one time, they kept a pen of rabbits in the backyard and sometimes ate rabbit stew, but that came to a skidding halt after Darlene was born ... she started naming the rabbits. She had a rabbit named Mollie who was afraid of thunder and would join Bobby's boxer, Satan, under the porch in a storm.

They also had some pet ducks named Donald, Huey, Dewey and Lewy, and the kids loved those ducks.

Dewey and Huey

One Easter Supper there was a big beautiful bird on the table. Billy asked, "Where's Huey?" and Bobby said, "We're eating him." Billy cried and carried on until Robert said, "Ah, the hell with it!" He got up from the table and threw the duck in the garbage. There was no Easter supper that year.

Donak Soup was one of the family favorites at the Swindell table. Tiny animals inside shells that could be found on the beach by sifting the sand with a Coke crate that had fine wire mesh on the bottom, the Donaks were boiled and a tasty, clear broth resulted. Then vegetables and other seafood could be added to make a delicious meal. Gladys also used to fix turtle stew, including the turtle eggs that were then so abundant on the beach and are now so carefully guarded by the Sea Turtle Patrols.

"We caught our fish and ate it all," recalls Billy. "It was free food when money was tight." Besides the obvious advantages, the family fishing adventures are fun to look back on. Robert and Gladys made crab cakes, fish chowder, fried or baked fish, oysters, eels and shrimp.

Often, the family would go to the beach with friends and relatives for a giant seafood and vegetable buffet – all fresh and delicious. Billy remembers that the men would line up with the tallest man first, and unroll the seine net into a half-moon shape, walking out into the surf as far as they could, scraping the bottom and catching everything the ocean had to offer. While the men were seining, the women and girls boiled water in huge cauldrons with all the seasonings and vegetables, waiting for the men to return with their catch. "Dad, being short, was one of the last to walk out, which was great for me because I got to sit on his shoulders," recalls Billy.

Speaking of fishing, Borum Outboard Boats were the "in" thing during the 1950's. Robert eventually got tired of renting little rickety rowboats and built a sturdy 16-foot wooden runabout with higher than normal sides so that he could fish the jetties without water coming into the boat. It had a 55-horsepower Scott Atwater Outboard Motor on it and was fast enough that the boys could ski behind it. He took them out skiing regularly.

Darlene remembers that Robert loved his little boat so much that he parked it in the garage instead of his car. "After one of the hurricanes hit (can't remember which one), we could have opened the garage door and the boat would have floated out," says Darlene. "That's how high the water was." After that hurricane, Gladys went to check on a neighbor who lived across a vacant lot from the house on Bee Street. Sloshing through the water, she stepped off the curb and went completely under. "Mother was only 4'11" tall," declares Darlene. "I think Billy had to go in and help her out of the water." One more side effect of that hurricane was the alligator that showed up the following week at Marjenhoff Park.

A family of many interests, the main one being the children, Robert and Gladys were avid sports fans, especially when one of their kids were involved. "Mom knew more about football and baseball than most men did," says Billy. Even when Robert was out of town, Gladys made sure to be in attendance at all of the athletic events where her children were involved.

Both Bobby and Billy went to Landon High School and played sports, Billy playing football and basketball, and Bobby playing football, baseball and basketball. Small and fast, Bobby won quite a bit of local fame as a halfback on Landon's football team, and made some points as a basketball player, too, although it was baseball that provided him with a Grant to the Citadel.

Landon's Bobby Swindell Selected 'Player Of Week'

When a 148-pound back barrels into a 200-pound line you'd expect him to bounce back a dozen feet.

But such was not the case with Landon's left halfback, Bobby Swindell, against the mammoth Jackson line last Friday.

He was instrumental in his club's three quick touchdowns which set Landon up for a 19-13 Big 10 victory and, as a result, is The Journal's selection for "Player of the Week."

In picking up 80 yards in 14 carries, a little less than half gained by the entire Landon backfield, Swindell led all ground gainers for the big intra-city clash.

Here's how Bobby figured in the Lion TDs:

He set up the first one with a 47-yard off-tackle smash that carried to Jackson's 16; passed to QG Mickey Dechman for 25 yards and the second TD and scored on an off-tackle smash that covered 11 yards for the third score. —JOE MOLONY

LANDON'S STAR RUNNER SET FOR MIAMI
HB Bobby Swindell to Start in GB Saturday

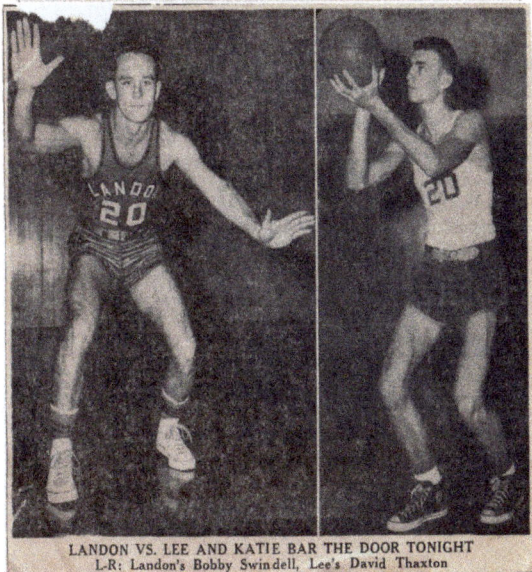

LANDON VS. LEE AND KATIE BAR THE DOOR TONIGHT
L-R: Landon's Bobby Swindell, Lee's David Thaxton

When he got to the Citadel, Bobby distinguished himself as a baseball player. He was known as "Lightning Fast Bobby Swindell" and would often be put into the game as a runner by his coach, who was passionate about winning. Bobby recalls one game when their coach was so elated that Bobby had stolen two bases and then gotten to home plate for the winning run that he nearly broke his favorite runner's neck! "The coach hugged me so hard that I ended up in the infirmary," laughs Bobby. "My fellow cadets kidded me about that one for years!"

During the summers, when Bobby was working with his Dad at the shipyard, he and Robert would get up at 3:30 a.m. to go to the beach for bait fish and back to one of the nearby creeks to fish until they had to leave for work at 7 a.m. Gladys always made sure her men had full bellies when they went off to fishing or work. For a brief time, when he was a senior at Landon, Bobby thought he might skip college. He was making $2.87 an hour, had a 1950 Willis automobile and a girlfriend. What more did a guy need? That decision was short-lived. Bobby graduated from The Citadel in Charleston, South Carolina, served in the U.S.

Marine Corps, and went on to enjoy a long and successful career in the printing industry.

Professional Profile
Bob Swindell

By KEN KEPLEY
Vice President, Palmer Paper Company

It is very difficult to express one's enthusiasm for his work, or his dedication to customer satisfaction but Bob Swindell, it seems to us, exemplifies those traits. So it wasn't surprising when Terry Brown asked *The Palmer Paper* to feature Bob in this May issue.

The excitement in Terry's voice as he described Bob was enough to convince us that Terry is thrilled to have Bob on board.

Bob started his career in the paper and graphic arts industries in January of 1966, in Jacksonville. He started at the ground floor working in the warehouse and subsequently moving into sales service. He was quickly promoted to a sales territory and has held a variety of sales and management positions since.

His career has been a distinguished one as he has received numerous awards including years of consecutive recognition

(Continued on page 10)

ROBERT L. SWINDELL JR. brings 19 years of experience in the paper and graphic arts industry to the staff of Palmer-Jacksonville.

Wide Experience Reported for Bob Swindell

(Continued from page 1)

for his achievements. When asked about his acceptance in the market, Bob expresses great appreciation to the customers who have supported him over the years.

Early in his career, he worked nights in print shops to gain an understanding of the craft and developed an invaluable orientation to the needs of the customers. He has been involved in many formal seminars and training experiences, including those of 3M, Kodak, Enco and Agfa in the graphic arts area and many mill visits to leading paper manufacturers including S. D. Warren.

"Palmer is the most exciting thing to happen to me in my 19 years in the business," Bob says. "The people here are fresh, knowledgeable, aggressive and intelligent. But what fascinates me most is their eagerness to satisfy the Number One need of our business: service to our customers.

"That combination, plus the excellent truly full service product line Palmer represents are the reason I'm here."

We at Palmer sincerely appreciate Bob's comments and we are equally enthusiastic about the attitude and experience he brings to Palmer.

Bob Swindell graduated in 1960 with a B.A. from The Citadel. He played varsity baseball and was a second lieutenant in the Marine Corps. In 1973 he completed some 15 hours of graduate study at the University of North Florida in business administration courses centering on management techniques in transportation and inventory control. He collects antiques and loves tennis, golf and fishing. He also has a pilot license and enjoys flying for pleasure when time permits.

Bob and his wife, Barbara, have two children, Chris, 23, a graduate in computer science from the University of Florida, and Carrie, 20, now a sophomore at the University of Florida. Barbara is successful as a real estate agent and owns her own company, Riverpoint Properties. She is also active in buying and selling antiques and appraising them.

Bobby, Citadel Cadet Summerall Guards

92

When Billy got old enough, he also went to work at the shipyards with his Dad, working the midnight to 7 a.m. shift. After a summer of this, Billy decided that blue collar work was not for him. He graduated from Florida State University, where he was a member of the ATΩ (ALPHA TAU OMEGA) Fraternity, and was Vice-President of his Pledge Class.

ATΩ Fraternity Party at FSU

Tall and good looking always, Billy has lived up to his mother's image of him and continues to be a handsome man with a ready smile, a warm personality, and a positive, insightful way of looking at the world.

Handsome Bill Swindell

After attending Daytona Beach Junior College and finishing up at Florida State University, graduating with a degree in Criminology, Billy was an MP (Military Policeman) in the Army, and then went into sales when he got out, working for Libby's Food Company for a while, where, in 1968, he was chosen Salesman of the Year in the Southeast and rewarded with full use of an automobile. At Zales Jewelry Chain, the largest retail jeweler in the world at that time, Bill was one of only two managers out of 750 nationwide who were recognized for excellence and rewarded with generous bonuses. He was featured in People Magazine's June 1983 issue, as follows:

Zales annual
FIRST & FINEST — Runner-Up Manager of the Year —

BILL SWINDELL
Store 1207, Regency Square,
Jacksonville, FL

If ever the term "super-sales-person" were to be used about one of our top Zale Division managers, surely you would apply it to our Runner-Up Manager of the Year, Bill Swindell.

Bill has come a remarkably long way in the short time he has been part of the Zales family, but then, Bill has always been a self-starter and a hard worker. Bill started out in a people-oriented business — working for himself — in a sandwich shop! Something about how to deal with the public must have rubbed off on him, because after leaving the food industry for the jewelry trade, Bill has gone right to the top of his field.

Since joining Zales in 1980, Bill has worked in Stores 275, Jacksonville, FL, and 894, Orange Park, FL, prior to being promoted to manager of Store 1207 in Jacksonville, Florida. A Florida native himself, Bill immediately took to the challenge of personal and store sales goals and began work as a rapidly excelling manager. His easy-going, yet thorough style of management has made Bill popular with both his employees and the public he serves so well.

Although Bill has certainly shown many strengths as a manager, everyone who knows him stresses his extraordinary capability in pure sales. In fact, his own personal sales records account for more than 40% of his store's monthly volume. That's pretty impressive in a store whose percentage of diamond sales and overall sales increase were among the best in the Division.

For Bill's accomplishments he will receive a check for $5,000.00 and our congratulations. His record speaks for itself as one of Zale Division leaders. His winning ways stand as a goal to which we all aspire.

Bill later worked as a State Farm Insurance Agent, retiring from that profession in 2008. Like his father, brother and sister, Billy has had a successful life, and spent most of it in his hometown of Jacksonville. Now retired, he keeps busy helping his wife, Arlene, a florist with a blooming business who keeps her husband busy decorating for weddings and special occasions throughout the year.

Back in 1996, on Pearl Harbor Day, both Bobby and Billy attended the Memorial Class, 205th Scottish Rite Reunion. The two brothers stood out from the crowd, both dressed in dark jackets and looking sharp on the right end of the 3rd Row in the group photo.

"Pearl Harbor" Memorial Class
205th Scottish Rite Reunion - December 7, 1996

After graduating from high school in 1968, Darlene went to Pensacola Junior College and became a dental assistant. She worked in dentistry for nearly 25 years, retiring when she married Jeff Spence in 1992. "Dad was insistent that all three of us go to college, although he always said that common sense would take you further than book-learning," says Darlene. "He's been a tough disciplinarian but he has always loved us and taken good care of us. He worked hard and wanted us to learn the value of hard work, too."

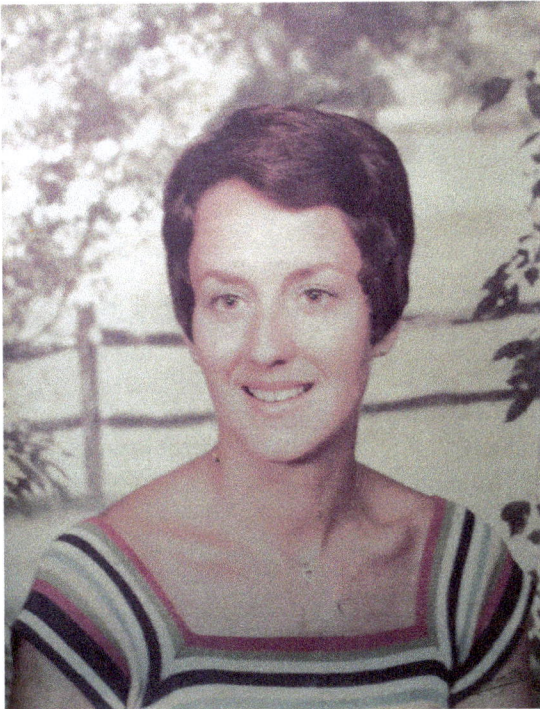

Darlene – High School

Robert always told Darlene that she looked just like her beautiful Aunt Mildred, and there was definitely a family resemblance, but he insists that he did not favor Darlene over her brothers. "I love all my children," he says. "They are good people." Looking at a photo of Darlene, Robert laughs out loud and reminisces about the time he and Gladys took her crabbing and she tripped and fell right into a crab bucket. "We had a lot of laughs when she was a little girl," he says, shaking his head and grinning.

Yes, laughter was prevalent at the house on Bee Street a great deal of the time, and while home brew accompanied many of the Swindell social and family times, drinking was not a major part of the fun.

**Gladys and Darlene perched on
the backyard barbeque**

CHAPTER 7
HERMIT'S COVE

When Robert retired from the shipyards, he wanted to get away from the city traffic and get to a place where he could relax and fish and just enjoy life. One of his good friends had found a nice, quiet place in Satsuma called Hermits Cove and so Robert and Gladys moved out there. Sadly, after only two years, their good friend died of cancer, but Robert and Gladys stayed. Robert loved Hermit's Cove.

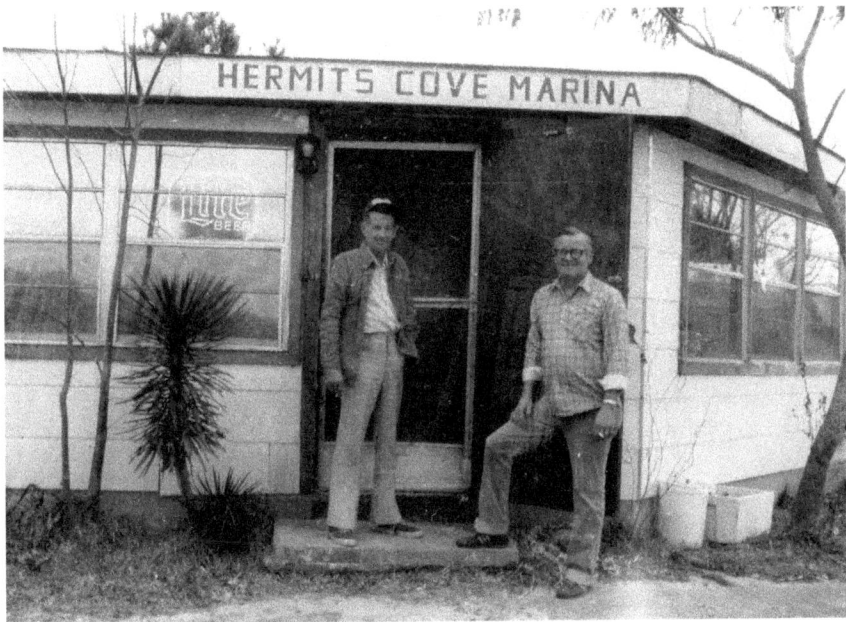

There was good fishing, he had his garden, he and Gladys still enjoyed dancing together and

there were some places nearby where they could go dancing ... or they could just cut the rug in their living room, as they had since they were young newly married teens.

Darlene was at work in the dental office one day when she called her mother to see how she was getting along in their new retirement place. "Oh, I'm alright," Gladys said, "Except for all these damn foreigners!" Foreigners? Darlene had heard about a big influx of Haitians that had come into Florida and she got worried. "Are the foreigners bothering you, Mother?" "Well, there are just so many of them," complained Gladys. "They're just everywhere and you know how I don't like them." Darlene was beginning to wonder if she should call her dad when Gladys explained that the "foreigners" were coming in daily from Detroit and other places up north to vacation at the UAW (United Auto Workers) trailer camp on the river nearby. The workers could come down and vacation for a nominal amount during the summer and, it turned out, they were the "damn foreigners" her mother had been talking about.

Gladys and Robert

In spite of those pesky foreigners, life was good at Hermit's Cove. Gladys and Robert enjoyed being together and were comfortable in their new place.

Robert, as always, loved doing the cooking, and Gladys didn't seem to mind at all that he had taken over that role in retirement.

Swindell Family - 1988

Darlene remembers that the ingredients for Sunday dinner at their place were always a bit of a mystery. One day an armadillo got into Robert's garden and the next thing they knew, it had been shot, cleaned and cooked on the grill for Sunday dinner. "If you wanted to know what you were going to be eating, you could always walk around the garden and find a shell of some sort or other evidence," Darlene says. "Sometimes it was better if you didn't know."

As the years went by and they got used to retirement, their three adult children and their families would come out to visit regularly and, as always, the joking would start. Now, though, with the kids all grown up, the jokes were sometimes on the parents. While David Larry had called his favorite cousin "Gladiola," the Swindell kids had their own nicknames for Gladys and Robert. "Glad-Ass" and "Raw-Butt!" Luckily, Gladys and Robert had the good humor to laugh ... after all, these were the children they had raised!

Gladys was not a complainer, but when she became ill with emphysema in 1988, she began to go downhill very quickly, losing weight and getting weaker. Darlene remembers that her mother had always been a small woman – never fat, but healthy and curvaceous. Now, she had become frail - just skin and bones. Darlene was dating Jeff Spence during the last two years of Gladys's life, but she didn't take him down to Hermit's Cove. It was just too painful to see her that way.

Toward the end, Gladys came down with a cold and went to the hospital in Palatka and within a matter of hours, it had gone into Pneumonia and she was moved to ICU. She was in a coma, in critical condition, for nearly a month. Robert stayed by her side in the hospital constantly. Darlene and Billy would drive down to Palatka nearly every day after work to give their dad a break – take him out to dinner or home for a shower. The doctor told them that if Gladys came home, she would be on oxygen and her quality of life would be nil.

"Dad was looking bad – starting to lose weight and look old. I told Billy that we had to do something or we'd lose them both." Darlene was sitting in Gladys's hospital room one night with Robert and she told her dad that she didn't feel this was a decision he could make because he was too close to Gladys. She said, gently, "She's been in a coma for weeks now and this is taking a toll on you, Dad. The doctors have already said she'll have no quality of life if she does come out of the coma ..." Robert told Darlene he'd think about what she'd said.

The very next morning, Darlene got a call at work. "You need to get down to the hospital immediately!" She walked in and her mother was sitting up in bed eating ice cream. She thought, "Oh my God, she heard me! She is showing me that there is no way I'm unplugging her. She's not ready to go. Am I in trouble now!" Later, when Gladys got home (without oxygen, no less) Darlene asked her if she had heard her and she swore she remembered nothing about the time she was in the coma. Darlene asked her if she'd seen the white light or the City of Gold, but again, she had no recollection of anything like that. She lasted about another year and then began to have some little mini-strokes, which ultimately led to her death on September 20, 1990.

Robert was lost. The love of his life was gone. He and Gladys had been together for more than half a century and he didn't know how to do life without her. Little by little, though, he began to realize that he was still a healthy, vigorous man and he couldn't spend the rest of his life in mourning. It was time for him to get back on the dance floor!

For a while, he played the field, a definite catch for some woman looking for a good man. Laverne Vaughn was secretary of the singles club in Palatka and loved to dance. They met at the Debonair Social Club in Palatka and from the first dance, it was as if they'd been dancing together forever. When Robert invited Laverne to a fish fry at his house in Satsuma, Laverne, a widow, talked to a friend of hers who was one of his neighbors.

"You met Robert Swindell?" exclaimed her friend. "He's one heck of a nice guy! He was good to his wife to the end."

At the time he first met Laverne, Robert had another lady friend who would come and visit him occasionally, but soon, it became obvious that he and Laverne were completely compatible, and she came to live with him at Hermit's Cove.

Robert & Laverne - 1992

Dancing was what they loved, and they danced whenever and wherever they could. Laverne was in her mid-50's when they met and her friends took one look at Robert and said, "Why, you've found a young man!" Age was never mentioned until one day they were at a cookout and a neighbor said, cattily, "You'd better ask him how old he is." She asked him and he said, "Does it really matter?" As it turned out, the fact that Robert is 19 years older than Laverne doesn't really matter in the least. They have loved one another for nearly 26 years and that's what matters.

Since they've been together, Robert and Laverne have literally danced their way around the country. In 2005, as Wyndham members, they traveled for six weeks, going to Ohio, West Virginia, Eerie, Pennsylvania, Nashville, Tennessee, Memphis, Texarkana, San Antonio, Niagra Falls, Ashevillle, North Carolina and elsewhere.

Laverne notes that although she has heard many moonshine and home-brew stories from Robert, she has never seen him drunk. "He has always been sober and a perfect gentleman," she says. "We've danced all over the United States and had a great time together!"

Speaking of great times, there have been several family stories added to the mix during the past quarter-century, many of them happening at Hermit's Cove in Satsuma. Once, when Bobby and Barbara and their children came by boat to Satsuma, they were all out on a canal and saw a snake. "Dad, get your gun," Bobby said. Robert sent Laverne back to the house to get the gun. Knowing nothing about guns, she looked down the barrel to see if it was loaded. "Give me that gun!" yelled Robert, glaring at Laverne and grabbing the gun. "Never look down the barrel of a gun … even if it's not loaded!" Robert, who was in the first stages of macular degeneration and was almost legally blind at the time, yelled, "Where's that snake?" He fired in the direction that Bobby pointed, missing the snake by two feet and scattering all of the occupants of the boat.

At Hermit's Cove, Laverne enjoyed reading, crocheting and knitting while Robert fished and cooked out. They had a pontoon boat that they would take down Dunns Creek, between Satsuma and Palatka. They grilled hot dogs and visited with neighbors across the canal. One day, Robert caught a 25-pound catfish and his neighbor, Wayne Bolin, was astonished at the size of it. He asked where Robert caught it so that maybe he could catch one to give to his mother-in-law. "Well, do you want this one?" Robert asked, simply handing him the fish.

One day, Robert came in and pointed at the neighbor's partial dock. He told Laverne, "There's a big log laying on the walkway. We need to go get it off." Laverne looked out and it wasn't a log. It was a big gator laying there in the sun! Robert's macular degeneration continued to degenerate, much to his dismay, but it didn't stop him.

Laverne was on the dock at Hermit's Cove and Robert laid his fishing pole down to go get something in the boathouse. It was dark in there and Laverne said she wasn't going in because she was afraid there might be a snake in there. "There's no snake!" yelled Robert, pulling back the door and revealing a large water moccasin. "Go get the gun!" he yelled. This one he did manage to hold up with a rake and shoot in the head.

"Robert never believes me," says Laverne. "We were checking a neighbor's boat and he raised up the cover and there was a moccasin underneath it. I told him to put the cover back. He looked at the moccasin and the moccasin looked at him – they were face to face – and then he put the cover back." When he hears that story, Robert shrugs. "He didn't bother me and I didn't bother him," he jokes. "We agreed not to bother each other."

Over the years, Robert's family came out to Hermit's Cove regularly to visit their Dad and Laverne, especially to celebrate birthdays, and one year the four Swindell men posed just alike for a classic photo.

"As far back as I can remember, Dad has almost always worn a hat," said Bobby, "and when a picture was being taken, he'd hook his thumbs in his belt, so I wore a hat like his and we all posed like Dad."

Billy, Robert, Bobby and Chris

**Gladys & Robert
Bee Street 1946**

**Robert, Gladys
& Darlene**

Darlene

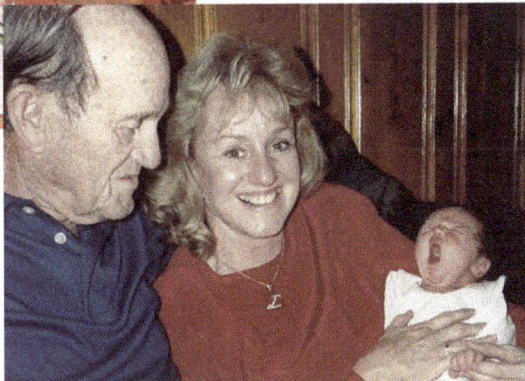

**Robert with Darlene and
her first grandson, Clay**

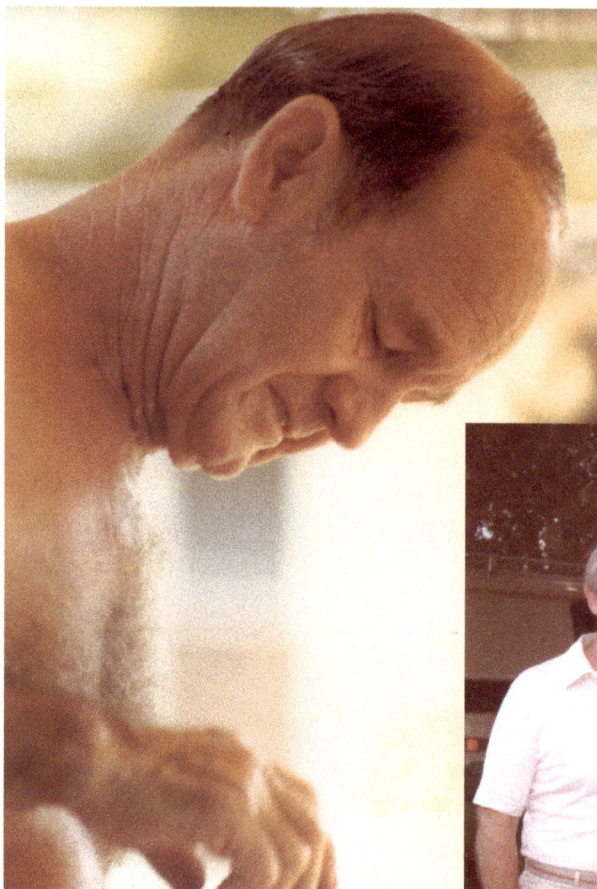

Robert

Bobby & Gladys
1975

Robert & Grandaughter Carrie

**Elizabeth & son, Hayden,
Robert & Jeff**

**Great grandchildren
Robby, Shannon & Zach
in France, 2015**

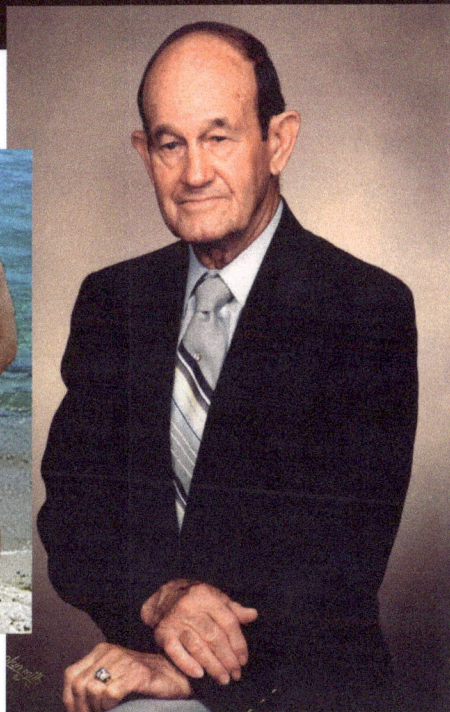

Robert

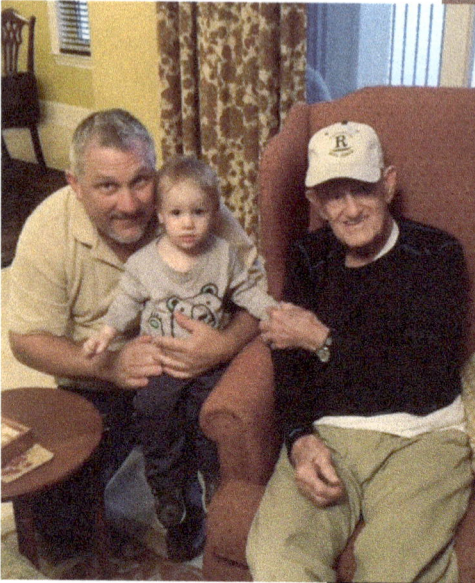

Jeff & grandson,
Oliver with Robert

Robert & Gladys

Elizabeth with
Carlton Spence

Robert & Darlene

Robert with
Donald Duck

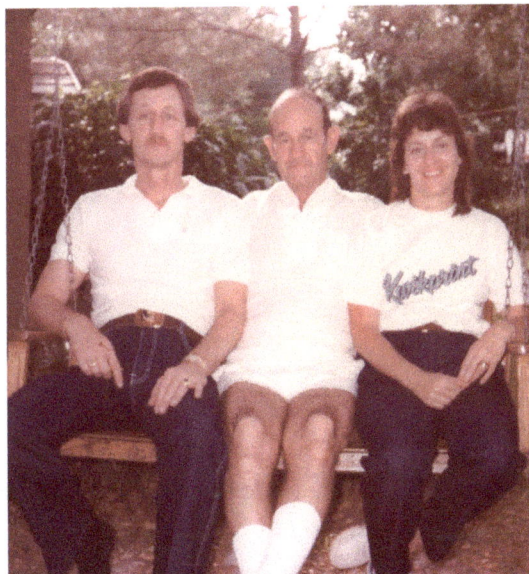

Billy, Robert & Darlene
at Hermit's Cove

Gladys's birthday
with Robert

Robert

Gladys & Robert
at Hermit's Cove

Sarah & Elizabeth

Lucky cat with Billy, Gladys & Darlene

Robert & Chance

**Robert & Gladys
with Tippy**

Billy, Gladys, Robert & Christine

**Darlene & Robert
at Hermit's Cove**

Barbara & Bobby

Bobby & Billy

Christina and Kayelynn

Shannon Atkins
Miss Bishop Kenny
2015-2016

FAMILY ALBUM

Billy, Arlene, Darlene & Jeff

Zach, Kathe & Chris, Robert & Barbara, Carrie, Shannon and Robby

Billy, Robert, Darlene & Bobby

CHAPTER 8
STILL DANCING!

Laverne & Robert still dancing in the living room - 2017

Darlene and Jeff once took a long trip to India several years ago and asked Robert and Laverne to house-sit his "Grand-Rabbit, Jimbo" at their home in Arlington. Darlene, who has loved animals all her life, had a big rabbit named Jimbo who lived in the house. They had a ritual with Jimbo that Darlene carefully explained to her Dad and Laverne. When it was time to go to bed, she would say to Jimbo, "Okay, let's go to bed." The rabbit would run through the house to his cage in the laundry room and sit up and wait for his cookie. He always had one Oreo Cookie before bed. Well, Robert and Laverne, thinking they'd save some money, bought Hydrox Cookies at the store instead of Oreo Cookies. After all, it was just for the rabbit. When they gave Jimbo the Hydrox Cookie, he threw it out of the room and would not eat and would not go in his cage. "Damn rabbit!" said Robert. "Now I have to go back and buy more cookies!"

Jeff and Darlene

When Jeff and Darlene returned from India,

Jimbo

Robert didn't tell her about the incident with Jimbo, but he did tell Darlene that he had some good news and some bad news. He had sold his house in Hermit's Cove, but the bad news was that he had one week to find a new place to live. Darlene and Jeff helped Robert find the new place in San Mateo – a beautiful piece of property on the water with a double-wide trailer where he and Laverne lived comfortably for several more years until they moved to Houston in 2014.

"We've had some great times with Dad at the little place in San Mateo," says Darlene. "It is in a great location and Dad stayed active there just about every day. I think that's one of the reasons he's lived so long is that he has always been active, and no one could ever tell him he couldn't do something – that just made it more important for him to do it."

Darlene's husband, Jeff Spence, grins when he recalls taking Robert and Laverne on a big family cruise to the Bahamas for Robert's 85th birthday. Their good friend, Rick Carter, owner of Holiday Adventures, Inc., booked the cruise and joined them for the fun. Rick was on shore when he ran into a large laughing Bahamian woman in the marketplace who was selling "We Be Jammin!" hats. He told the woman that his friend, Robert, was celebrating his 85th birthday and pointed him out to her, surreptitiously buying one of the hats and asking her to pretend she was presenting it to the "birthday boy" as a gift because she was so taken with him and so awed by his youthful appearance. The woman outdid herself, fawning over Robert, who was absolutely amazed that this huge black woman seemed to smitten with him. She went on and on for quite a while and then made a big ceremony of placing the hat on his head. For the remainder of the cruise, Robert was nicknamed "We Be Jammin!" by the family, and Rick Carter still calls him that whenever he sees him.

Since Robert and Laverne moved to Houston to live with Laverne's daughter, Shirley, Shirley's

Bobby and Mark discussing Damn Tree (San Mateo)

husband Jim, and Laverne's sons, Wesley and Randall, the home in San Mateo has sat vacant, but the grounds have been kept up and taxes paid by Bobby, Billy and Darlene. One day in February, Bobby was out at the property at the same time the groundskeeper, Mark Manning, was there, and Mark recounted one of his favorite stories about Robert's determination to do what he is going to do ... no matter what! Mark came one day to take care of the yard and trim the trees and do the monthly maintenance on the grounds. "I have a few customers that I really look forward to seeing," said Mark,

129

"and one of them is Mr. Swindell. He's just got some great stories to tell and sometimes we just sit and talk out here for an hour or so." That day, though, Robert had Mark worried. As he pulled up and got out of his truck, he spotted Robert hobbling across the yard, bent nearly double and rubbing his back as if he was in pain. Mark went over to him and asked if he could help. "Naw, I'm going to be fine," insisted Robert. "I just fell out of that damn tree, that's all!" It turned out that Robert had been preparing for Mark's visit to help him by getting up in the tree to sweep the leaves and debris off the roof so Mark wouldn't have to do that! "I couldn't believe it!" Mark told Bobby, pointing up at the tree. "I don't even want to climb that tree!"

Darlene wasn't surprised to hear about her Dad climbing that "damn tree." She noted that he had been up on the roof of the boathouse several times and had actually fallen, fully clothed, into the water from the dock, but somehow, never really hurt himself. "He's so strong," she marvels. "He's always been disciplined about his eating habits and so active that he has just stayed in great shape.

130

He really enjoyed being out at that property and he never seemed to stop. We had some good times there."

When Laverne thinks of good times, she especially recalls the cruise she and Robert took to the Bahamas on Jeff and Darlene's big boat. They stayed on it for about a month and had the time of their lives.

"Darlene kept gathering all the food scraps in a big pot," recalls Laverne. "I asked her why and she said, 'You'll see.'" We went out in their motor boat and there were wild pigs swimming out to eat the scraps! Really! I've never seen anything like it!"

Then, as if that wasn't enough excitement, Laverne talks about how Jeff dove into the beautiful water and brought up a starfish. What a grand adventure that cruise was!

Laverne and Robert – Starfish

Once in a while, Robert and Laverne still dance together whether on a cruise or in their living room. As long as he's upright, Robert will dance.

Today, having reached the century-mark in his life, Robert lives in a large home in Houston with Laverne and her family, which includes five little Chihuahua's ... no danger of Asthma there! He spends a great deal of time listening to audio-books from the Houston Library and has read and re-read every Louis L'amour and John D. MacDonald book ever written. He walks unassisted and upright without a cane, and nearly always wears a hat of some sort. Although he is legally blind from macular degeneration and his hearing has deteriorated greatly, Robert lights up when he hears good music and he still loves a good joke.

When asked to what he attributes his longevity, Robert grins and squints his eyes, thinking long and hard before he answers.

"In my earlier years, I think that white lightning spurred me on," he says. "I guess that's one secret to my long life. Then I had to stay healthy to take care of Gladys and my kids for all those years..." About this time, Laverne pipes up, "I kept him on his toes!" Robert nods his head. "She sure did! She kept me dancing.

What was it about those Moonshine Days that spurred young Robert Lee Swindell on to move up in the world, live a long and fulfilling life and become an expert at just about everything he's ever done? "Ah hell," he says, "I just knew that white lightning was temporary ... I had a lot more to do and I did it."

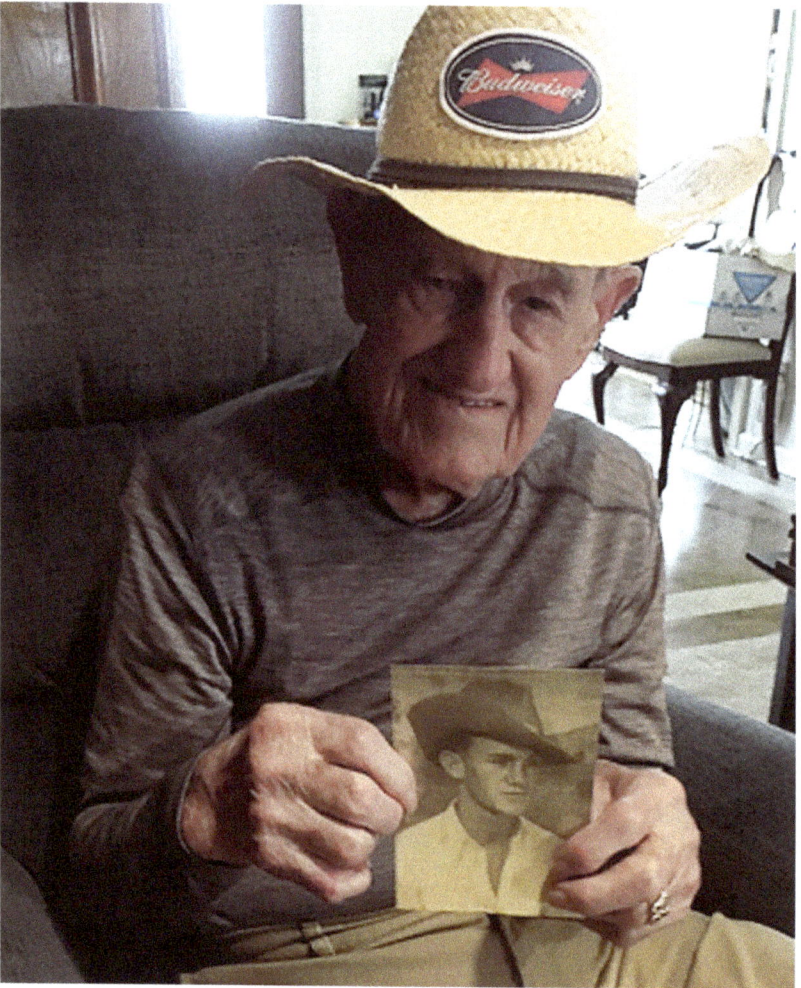

Robert ... Young and Old – Still Handsome!

ANCESTRY OF ROBERT LEE SWINDELL

SWINDELL FAMILY

Doc Swindell married Janie Yarbrough
      (b. 1863-d. 1935) (buried in Anthony, FL)
Daughters: Agnes and Ola
Sons:
    William Henry m. Florence Sims
      Daughters:
        Ula (Higginbotham)
        Thelma (Ross)
        Myrtle
    Robert David m. Eva Annise (Ann) Howard
      Daughter: Mildred (b. 1918-d. 1956)
      Son: **Robert Lee Swindell** (b. May 15, 1916)
        m. Eva Gladys Olson (b. Aug. 24, 1918 –
        d. Sept. 22, 1990)
    Robert & Gladys had three children:
      Son: Robert Lee, Jr. (Bobby)
        m. Barbara Wilson
        Daughter: Carrie
          Daughter: Shannon Lane
          Son: Robert Michael
        Son: Chris
          Daughter: Lauren Panda
          Son: Zach Lee Swindell
      Son: William Henry, II. m. Arlene
        Daughter - Christina
        Daughter: Jennifer
      Daughter: Ellen Darlene m. Jeff Spence
        Daughter: Elizabeth Hope
        Daughter: Sarah

OLSON FAMILY

(Immigrated through Boston)

Julius Olson m. Emma Pomeroy (who lived to be 103)

Daughters:

Margaret m. Paul Cordele

Irene m. Henry O'dell

Thelma m. Wilbur Larry

Son: David Larry m. Sharon

Sons:

Cecil Olson m. Peggy

Bowen Daniel Olson m. Eva Smith

Daughter:

Eva Gladys m. **Robert Lee Swindell**

Sons:

Bowen Daniel, Jr. (B.D.) m. Mildred Swindell

Leslie m. Frances

HOWARD FAMILY

Matthew Napoleon Howard, born Sept. 3, 1868, married Lily Harper, b. May 4, 1880, on December 19, 1894. Lily was the daughter of Thornton Floyd Harper, who lived to be 110 years old and was the grandfather of Eva Ann Howard, who married Robert David Swindell, son of Doc and Jane (Yarbrough) Swindell. An article ran on March 29, 1946 in the Lake City and Columbia Gazette about Columbia's Oldest Resident – Floyd Harper. Born on the 4th of May, 1836, his Death Certificate indicates that Thornton Floyd Harper died on August 5th,

Thornton Floyd Harper, 107th Birthday

COLUMBIA'S OLDEST RESIDENT

—Floyd Harper Lived Here 101 Years—

RECALLS EARLIEST DAYS HERE

Columbia county's oldest citizen celebrated a birthday Thursday last week at the home of his daughter, Mrs. Rosa Markham. He is Mr. Thornton Floyd Harper and it is established that he has lived in what is now Lake City for 101 years. He was born in North Carolina and the fact that he came here when nine years of ago indicates that he is now 110 years old.

Mr. Harper attributes his longevity to hard work. Up until two years ago he was able to cut wood. For the past week he has been indisposed and confined to his bed, which was the case when relatives and friends in great numbers came to pay their respects on his birthday.

Of bright eye and clear memory Mr. Harper can talk interestingly of the olden days in this section. Life was simple indeed, in the early days, as compared to the complexities of today's civilization.

His first recollections are of a settlement known as Alligator. It was named, according to Mr. Harper, after an unfriendly Indian chief. It was not until about eight years after the Civil War that the name was changed to Lake City. There were four families when Mr. Harper first came here. Growth of the section was slow so that during the Civil War it had only increased to about three dozen households.

Game was bountiful in woods, streams and lakes. Crops were easy to make and the only "imports" were coffee and flour. A trip to Jacksonville, which usually took two days and nights to make, became necessary every so often to obtain these essentials. Flour, by the way, was five dollars a barrel in those good old days and the barrel made a good chair or liquid receptacle. Big Lake was full of fish so that a 'mess' could be obtained at any time in about an hour. They were gigged, usually with a pitchfork. Turkeys were almost tame and venison, fresh and smoked, was a staple part of the daily diet. There were good and bad Indians just like other folks.

Weather was warm all the time in those early days too. Frost was practically unknown but Mr. Harper had no explanation as to the whys and wherefores of the change.

Lake City and Columbia county did not really begin to grow until after the Civil War when woodsmen's axes and the whining saws of the mills began to flourish. Then expansion of the town and country took place. And, frankly, while he did not say so, it was indicated he enjoyed best the good old days of Alligator and East Florida.

138

1946, making him 110 years and 4 months old at the time of death. His granddaughter, Eva, b. May 20, 1900, was the mother of our own 100-year-old hero, Robert Lee Swindell.

On March 2, 2017, Susan and Tom Howard of Lake City contributed to this biography by sharing photos and memories of Thornton Floyd Harper, as well as the newspaper clipping mentioned above.

Tom and Susan Howard

Tom Howard was at his great-grandfather's 107th birthday at Aunt Rosa Markham's house and he remembered how active and spry Harper was at that age. Tom talked of his great-grandfather sitting on the front porch and regaling the young children of the family with exciting stories of Old Chief Alligator of the Seminole Tribe, and how General Andrew Jackson came to kill the Chief and the Indian barely escaped with his life, running south six miles by the "Big Lake" and past the Santa Fe River all the way to Camp Olena. On the day that Great-Grandfather Harper presented his cousin Beau with a 22 rifle, Tom was right there, and at 88, he still talked a bit resentfully of how he had really wanted that rifle for himself. Tom remembered Great-Grandpa Harper talking of taking produce to Cowford (now Jacksonville) in exchange for flour and dry goods.

Tom and Susan Howard were cordial, and happy to help with Robert's biography, expressing great affection for him and wishing him well on his 101st birthday coming up in May 2017. Grinning broadly, Tom noted that his 89th birthday was just around the corner and he was feeling well and looking forward to it.

Sadly, due to a stroke, Tom Howard died on March 25th, just a few weeks after contributing to this book. We are grateful for Tom's contribution and we send our condolences to Susan Howard in Lake City and the rest of their family.

Carpe' Diem! Seize the Day ... we never know what tomorrow holds.

www.ingramcontent.com/pod-product-compliance
Lightning Source LLC
Chambersburg PA
CBHW040418110426

42813CB00013B/2694